A WALK IN
THE WOODS

Exploring Britain's Greatest Woodland

WOODLAND
TRUST

A WALK IN

Archie Miles

THE WOODS

Exploring Britain's Greatest Woodland

FRANCES LINCOLN LIMITED
PUBLISHERS

THIS BOOK IS
DEDICATED TO
MY LATE FATHER,
RALEIGH MILES
(1912-1971)

An antiquarian book
seller all his working
life, with a prodigious
knowledge of his chosen
field, he inspired my
abiding love of books
and sowed the seeds of
my passion for natural
history. Sadly, he never
lived long enough to
see me in print, but I
hope that he would have
approved of what I do.

Frances Lincoln Ltd
4 Torriano Mews
Torriano Avenue
London NW5 2RZ
www.franceslincoln.com

A Walk in the Woods
Copyright © Frances Lincoln 2009
Text copyright © Archie Miles 2009
Photographs copyright © Archie Miles
First Frances Lincoln edition: 2009

A catalogue record for this book is
available from the British Library.

ISBN 978-0-7112-2957-0

Printed and bound in China

9 8 7 6 5 4 3 2 1

HALF TITLE PAGE Old beech
pollards beneath the glowing
emerald canopy of May in
Savernake Forest

TITLE PAGE View north out of
Nant Gwynant towards the
Watkin path up Snowdon,
whose dark summit peers over
the skyline.

RIGHT The intricate detail of
an ancient sweet chestnut bole
at Croft.

CONTENTS

The seasons are a constant source of fascination. I often revisit the same tree or wood many times to see the changes wrought by variations in the weather and the seasons, and even the quality of light at different times of day. I barely noticed this stunning field maple during a summer visit, but upon my return in October the tree leapt from the landscape, demanding to be photographed. How could I resist?

When I was a little lad – and by little I mean before I was eleven years old and had to go to big school, which involved lots of homework and preparation for exams and all that nearly-grown-up onerous sort of stuff – I would spend a very large part of my time roaming the countryside, with my gang of mates, around the Yorkshire village where I was brought up. Gang should not be taken as a rough bunch of ne'er-do-wells armed with offensive weapons, but more a band of brothers with the occasional big stick, muddy knees, ripped shorts and a constant yearning for sweets, fizzy pop and adventure.

Come rain or shine we'd be off after breakfast and seldom home until the sun went down. We were lucky, for we had the whole of Ilkley Moor as our adventure playground, but it's remarkable to recall how much time we spent in the woods. I probably wasn't aware of it at the time, but I think we felt safe in the woods; it was our own private world where we built our dens or hides, had our own games and our own rules, and woe betide those who would interfere. Sometimes there were elements of tribalism, when petty territorial disputes erupted with kids from other gangs or neighbouring villages. The worst it came to was usually a few bruises, a lot of catcalling and backchat and perhaps the theft of someone's climbing rope or ladder. Differences could be sorted or leadership asserted by proving you could jump down from a higher tree branch than your challenger, or simply climb to the topmost branch of some ridiculously high tree without losing your nerve. We played games which involved hunting, tracking and hiding – it might have been Japs and Commandos, Cowboys and Indians or even, as it should have been, Robin Hood and the Sheriff of Nottingham (after all, Richard Greene was our hero every week in glorious black and white). We knew the plants and berries that we could and couldn't eat. We knew nettle from dead-nettle. We made blowpipes and pea-shooters from elder twigs. We built camp fires to keep us warm on cold days and cooked spuds, which we'd pinched from Mum's veg box, in the embers. In essence, although we never gave it a second thought, we were in tune with the natural world around us.

The seeds were sown. A childhood blessed by my parents' affection for nature, and their desire to share their own knowledge and fascination, was certainly a great start, and I think that being immersed in woodland for so much of the time meant that it was simply and subliminally absorbed into my system. The woodland in me lay dormant, only to germinate about fifteen years ago as trees began to re-emerge as a significant influence and interest in my life.

At present, when there are so many different influences and attractions on offer to children, many of which don't necessarily involve getting out and about, it's good to find that the Woodland Trust has come up with some great ideas to get young people excited about trees and woodland. The Nature Detectives website (www.naturedetectives. org.uk) has 101 ways to turn a woodland visit into an adventure, and the Ancient Tree Hunt (www. AncientTreeHunt.org.uk) will turn kids on to the tree monsters hidden all over the country . . . with a few hugs along the way. A wide variety of woodland events are available throughout the year provided by several different organizations. Among these the National Trust, Forestry Commission and the local Wildlife Trusts all offer programmes of special activities; and the Tree Council promotes its Walk in the Woods campaign each May, with walks, talks and much more all over Britain.

Woodland is an ever-present element of the British landscape wherever you live; and wherever that happens to be your local woods may be a greater or lesser element in your own 'terra familia'. The woodland cover has been evolving for the last 10,000 years and it's still in a constant state of flux today. In the past countless woods have been felled or grubbed out. Thankfully, that is now happening less and less, and on the positive side woods are being planted; sometimes conifers, but also many broadleaved trees, and on a grand scale too. Every region, every different terrain and climate generates its own specialized types of woodland; and these have been classified and divided into seventy-five different sorts or stands; and that just covers our ancient woodlands: those that have been established since before 1600. Some are slight variations of closely allied types, but perhaps occurring on different soils, at different altitudes, or with a preponderance of one species rather than another, a different shrub layer or specific flora, and so on. Then, of course, there are all the woods of introduced species, mainly conifers, most of which might be adequately described as plantations, but even so they acquire their own specific ecosystems and habitats. What is amazing about Britain is that we have so much variation among our woodlands within the confines of a relatively small island. Travel 20 or 30 miles in different directions and you'll inevitably find different types of woods.

This book will not burden you with every last detail of all the different woodland types throughout Britain, but it will make you aware of the great diversity and beauty of our woods and their associated landscapes. The hope is that you'll be encouraged to get out there, to explore and enjoy these woods, learn a bit about them, understand their natural evolution, their importance to wildlife and their place in the overall scheme of our social and cultural history. Once you have visited these ones, you will have merely skimmed the surface, dipped a toe in the water, but the intention is that you'll be inspired to go and visit many of the other sites listed in the gazetteer; then perhaps pick up the regional *Exploring Woodland Guides* to expand your options even further. You may even discover your own special woodland places … some of which might not be in anyone's guidebook.

In the following pages you'll be introduced to all kinds of different woodland, including sites from all over Britain. Selecting the sites was often difficult, but eventually the choices were made; sometimes on the basis of the principal tree species in the wood; sometimes for their specific landscape features; while various social, cultural and industrial associations made others absolute winners.

There are so many superb oak woods and beech woods all over Britain that focusing on just two of each of these was particularly tricky. You may feel that your favourite should have pipped our selections at the post, but on offer for your delectation are a superb coppice oak wood alongside an ancient wood pasture full of gnarled old pollards. And it's

I am intrigued by trees and their relationships with the landscapes they inhabit, seeking connections with the elements of chance arrival and survival; inseparable from the formidable forces of nature – light and shade, earth, rock, wind and water – and the manner in which every individual tree responds. Discovering bizarre forms or anthropomorphic manifestations, typified by this strange old beech in Coed Tyn-y-gelli, throws my senses of reason and sanity into question, but it's exciting and crazy all at once. Such wayward imaginings fire my passion for trees.

not just the trees, but also the stories that revolve around them – some of the initial investigations into dendrochronology in Britain began at the ancient oaks of Lochwood in Dumfries & Galloway. Burnham Beeches in Buckinghamshire simply can't be overlooked, for where else could you find such a wonderful community of beechen geriatrics? Savernake Forest in Wiltshire blends old, outgrown pollards with young beech forestry and the longest beech-lined avenue in Britain; a legacy from the attentions of the great Lancelot 'Capability' Brown in the eighteenth century.

Sweet chestnut, although a frequent feature of broadleaved woods throughout Britain, deserves most note for its impressive coppice woods of England's south-east counties. Again, yew is a tree with national distribution, occurring particularly in woods on chalk and limestone. The choice is immense, but only a handful of woods have large dominant stands of yew and, of these, Kingley Vale jumps to the fore as the finest yew wood in Europe.

The limestone theme leads seamlessly to both the woods with native limes: the network of sites around Bardney in Lincolnshire and the great old veteran trees being rediscovered in the Wye Valley. The whole saga of the native lime is a heartwarming story of a neglected broadleaved tree, which some 5,000 years ago was one of the dominant species of British lowland woods. In the wake of climate change its presence slowly receded, and only through human influence, by coppicing and pollarding, did lime hang on to its place in the national silva. Native limes are also present in many of the woods growing on limestone. Eaves Wood weaves a cautious trek across the limestone pavement around Silverdale, at the northern tip of Lancashire; while Ebbor Gorge, which cuts a deep gash through the Mendips of Somerset, opens up distant views across the Levels. Ever onward to the ravine woods, where the raging torrents and dramatic falls of the Mellte and Hepste rivers carve their way through Coed-y-Rhaiadr, above Neath; and, away up on the coast of County Durham, Castle Eden Dene has gouged its own impressive course to the sea over thousands of years.

Castle Eden Dene bridges the gap between ravine and coastal wood, and typically, wherever there are deep defiles running down to the coast, they will provide protection for trees to grow in steep impenetrable sites, which have historically been useless for agriculture, grazing and even a little dodgy for timber extraction. Oak comes to the fore again in the estuarine woods of Kilminorth in Cornwall – it seems to be a Cornish thing the way oaks thrive in these tidal estuaries, their boughs trailing in the high tides and some of their roots undoubtedly immersed in brackish water. In the north-west of England you'll find Sea Wood (rather obvious name), whose lower reaches look a bit like an arboreal lemming horde about to leap off their limestone cliff into the sea.

The west coast of Britain has a great natural gift to its treescapes, namely the presence of the Gulf Stream, which has helped to maintain warm wet conditions for thousands of years, making the Atlantic oak woods incredibly rich repositories for mosses, ferns and lichens. There's a glimpse at Sunart in the West Highlands of Scotland and Nant Gwynant in Snowdonia. Alder also does extremely well in these western woods, but discovering alder carr woods, an increasingly rare woodland type due to widespread agricultural drainage programmes, is getting much harder. Coed y Cerrig, near Abergavenny, shows you exactly how splendid these primeval-looking, swampy glades can be – and there's a nifty boardwalk to bear you safely above the mire. Over in Lincolnshire, Tattershall Carrs, with its monster alder coppice stools, gives a little insight into what must have been lost already in so many woods in eastern England.

Tattershall also lends its association to the famous 'Dambusters' squadron, who flew from nearby RAF Woodhall Spa, with many of the old billets and air-raid shelters still within the woodland. Evidence of industrial history lurks beneath the surface of many a wood, for wherever there was coppicing there was usually charcoal burning (the old pitsteads often still discernible) and bark peeling. Benthall Edge Wood, near Ironbridge, reveals traces of mining for coal and quarrying for limestone, ironstone, sandstone and clay around this vibrant powerhouse of the Industrial Revolution. Whittle Dene, in the peaceful Northumbrian countryside, hides crumbling remains of an old water mill, which ground its last flour over a century ago.

Britain's landowners have left their indelible marks on our wooded landscapes. Hackfall, in North Yorkshire, was an eighteenth-century created 'wilderness' complete with romantic follies, grottoes and surprise vistas. For most of the twentieth century it languished, but a full and sensitive restoration programme is gently putting the original spirit back into this celebrated (and Grade 1 listed) woodland garden. In the early nineteenth century in Staffordshire the 15th Earl of Shrewsbury was already engrossed with his gardening magnum opus at Alton Towers, when he clapped eyes on Dimmings Dale, on the edge of his estate, and coveted this as his own little stretch of tamed wilderness with which to entertain guests. The river was dammed, ponds were formed, trees were planted and a broad carriageway built. Today you may stroll through a wealthy man's rural idyll, abandoned to the forces of nature.

The parklands around the grand houses of the gentry have bequeathed us a phenomenal heritage of ancient trees, many of which were absorbed from ancient woodland or hedgerows into formal schemes by the great landscapers. There are specimen trees planted for ornament or ostentation, some native and some the latest arrivals – in the mid-nineteenth century who would dare to be seen without a wellingtonia or a monkey puzzle? There were woodland clumps planted to appear 'natural'; avenues that were sometimes fashionable and sometimes not; woodland specifically for game cover. The choice is massive – you get a peek at Ickworth Park in Suffolk and Croft Castle in Herefordshire (my local and all-time favourite tree parkland – the sweet chestnuts are jaw-droppingly wonderful).

There's more, lots more, but there have to be a few surprises for you along the way. The hope is that you will be inspired to venture forth into the woods. Even if it just means taking a closer look at your local woods, get out there at different times of year, in different weather, at sunrise or sunset. You'll be amazed how the same place, which you thought you knew so well, can take on so many different guises.

Watch for winter days when hoar-frost descends – be quick, as it soon melts – but at its best you'll think the winter wood has suddenly thrown a flush of white leaves. Wrap up warm and crunch through newly fallen snow, searching for animal spoors. Don't forget to stuff an identification guide in your pocket so you know what you've found – you'll never believe how many deer are in your wood … and you've never seen a single one.

In springtime get up early – go and sit in the wood before the sun comes up, and listen to the dawn chorus. It will blow you away, and with luck you'll also get to see owls and bats returning to roost from their nightly hunting forays. After dark the honeysuckle smells even sweeter, as it lures night-flying moths to its exotic flowers. The intense aroma of massed bluebells can be almost overpowering, but it is sweet indeed when compared to the peppery stench of wild garlic.

Summer brings long hot days (hopefully) when the woods now provide valuable shade, an aspect which may well gain more prominence as our climate warms. In the glades and rides butterflies flit happily among the flowers, particularly where management such as coppicing has opened up woodland clearings – great for the wildlife … and the perfect setting for a picnic.

In autumn it's all down to the colours. Beech woods always look stunning, particularly when backlit by low sunlight, but for the richest hues seek out field maple, rowan, birch and aspen. Where the latter two species dominate, on Deeside and Speyside in Scotland, late October is a massive colour-fest. Fungus forays are great fun at this time, but make doubly sure you know exactly what you're picking and, moreover, eating. Enjoy the wet, pungent smell of autumn leaves, and the rhythmic shushing as you march on through drift after drift.

So, what does the future hold for Britain's woodland? It's startling to realize that although about 12 per cent of the country is wooded, only 2 per cent is ancient woodland. It is also a sobering thought to learn that Britain has lost nearly 50 per cent of the ancient woodland that existed in the 1930s, mainly to agriculture, development and non-native conifers. From its inception in 1972, the Woodland Trust has worked hard to improve and reverse these desperate trends for our native woods, and with very impressive results. Among its achievements, it has planted more than 8 million native trees; currently cares for more than 1,100 woods, covering 50,000 acres; and has created almost 8,000 acres of new native woodland.

Commendable as that may be, as the Trust knows only too well, there's no time for inactivity or complacency. An exciting new project, just beginning in Hertfordshire, is set to see the formation of England's largest new native woodland – Heartwood Forest will eventually cover a stupendous 850 acres. In Scotland, the 12,000 acres of the Trust's Glen Finglas Estate will soon become integrated with the Great Trossachs Forest, and in Wales the Plant! initiative has been launched with the aim of planting a native tree for every baby born in Wales.

This little oak tree may not be the most impressive or imposing specimen that I have ever photographed. When I came across it in a tiny clearing in the depths of Wentwood Forest it seemed a potent symbol in the context of this ancient forest, which is only just beginning to emerge from its dreary, smothering blanket of conifers. Bathed in sunlight, the tree flourishes and, for a moment, I can capture the exuberance of its success. Ultimately it's all about light, for without it there is no life, and without either of these there is no image.

Across Britain the Tree For All campaign is working to involve 2 million children in the planting of 12 million trees … and they're well on the way. The ultimate goal is to see our native woodland cover doubled by 2050.

After that rollercoaster ride of woods to visit and woods to cherish, and even the prospects of woods for the future, what exactly is it that makes them such special places? What is that intangible, mysterious reason why woods feel so right?

Many people have said that standing in a cathedral evokes an overwhelming sense of spirituality, humility and wonder. I have experienced similar emotions in cathedrals, but I haven't necessarily found that comforting, uplifting or reassuring. Mostly, I feel a sense of admiration for the masons and craftsmen of old; an incredulity at the enormous scale of design and construction. While appreciating what they are, they do nothing for my soul. Comparisons are often drawn between cathedrals and monumental groves of trees. The trees do it for me; the stones do not. I find that I have no spiritual allegiance to any religious persuasion, although if I were forced to acknowledge some deity, it would be the innate life-force of nature itself. The enigmatic yew tree guards its secrets of growth, of ageing and the spiritual reasons why it has been allowed to grow or was planted where we see it today. I find that mystery thought-provoking and uplifting and yet, while I am intrigued, I hope the mystery will endure. When we understand everything, what is left? So, perhaps it is right that there is no easy explanation to the euphoria of woodland. My wild, roaming childhood helps me enjoy being in the woods, and what I have learnt over the years helps me to understand their evolution and structure, but ultimately there is no simple, all-encompassing answer to why woods are so special. Experience woodland and love it for how it makes you feel. It is enough.

The essayist and novelist John Berger encapsulates a sense of the woods to which I can relate:

> Even when working in the forest alone, one has an elusive sense of company. A flat field, a bare hillside, or the steppe are not the same. The trees constitute a presence. They maintain – each according to its species – an extraordinary balance between movement and stillness, between action and passivity. And in this balance, all the while being regulated, their presence is palpable.

TREES ON THE BRINK

CASTLE EDEN DENE

Dramatic ravine woodland cuts down to the Durham coast

The stunning 4-mile-long gorge of Castle Eden Dene, cut deep through the Magnesian limestone of coastal County Durham, boasts the largest ancient woodland in north-east England. Like a forgotten, hidden fold in the fabric of this sparsely wooded landscape, the gorge lies surprisingly close to the modern sprawl of the town of Peterlee. In fact it has sometimes been described as the town's back garden. For the last twenty years or so this National Nature Reserve has been in the trusty hands of Natural England (and its predecessors), which keeps the 12 miles of footpaths here, ranging over 550 acres, carefully maintained while also managing the woodland in the best interests of flora and fauna.

For more than 150 years Castle Eden Dene has been the resort of tourists and naturalists seeking a sylvan wilderness to inspire and fascinate. In the nineteenth century it was known as Castle Eden Dean, the Saxon *den* or *dene* simply signifying a wooded valley. In the twelfth century a castle stood above the Dene, but in the 1760s the Newcastle financier, Rowland Burdon, built a fine Neo-Gothic house upon the site. Castle Eden Hall survives to this day. The Dene was all part of his extensive estate and a fitting wilderness garden for his splendid new home. In the 1790s Burdon's son (also named Rowland . . . as was every eldest son for seven generations) began to construct paths and bridges to make the valley accessible. In 1850 the Dene was first opened up for the enjoyment and wonder of those Victorians with a thirst for romantic and rugged scenery. They could ramble to their hearts' content or view the delights of the gorge from the comfort of their carriage.

There are several flowery accounts of the period, often accompanied by fine engravings where elegant folk perambulate or pause in decorous groups to admire the view or take refreshments. The lyricist Joseph Blackett, finding himself 'in the centre of one

OPPOSITE The twisted and contorted roots of the yews in the Dene are an endless source of wonder. Decked with ivy and set among the glossy leaves of hart's tongue fern, this tree appears to be 'devouring' a lump of rock.

BELOW Young ash and wych elm strive upwards for the sunlight from the fern-clad floor of Castle Eden Dene.

A fine engraving by Thomas Allom, from 1833, perfectly illustrates the densely wooded nature of Castle Eden Dene. Visitors perambulate and picnic along one of the rides, while Castle Eden Hall rises above the woods on the far side of the ravine.

of the wildest glens mine eyes ever beheld' in 1809, was moved to write:

Judge of my rapture, and share the transport which I then experienced. From the shelving sides of regularly sloping rocks, hung trees of all hues; the light green youthful ash, the sombre yew, the sun-burnt beech, and the dark holly, formed to the eye the finest contrast of colours imaginable. Mine eyes dwelt on this scene with delight; and shortly after, witnessed another with astonishment and awe – for piercing through the bosom of the Dean in a western direction, and clambering over some precipices, I came to a horrid chasm, through which the waters rushed with a force that made the adjacent perforated rocks, re-bellow to the roar. This is the true sublime of scenery, said I …

Today the scenery has changed little; in truth it has probably changed very little in the last 10,000 years. The combination of boulder clay overlying the limestone has been etched by the continuous action of water down the millennia, sculpting the overhanging cliffs and forming numerous caves and hollows; underground hollows so deep that the rushing torrents of winter dwindle to a mere trickle by spring and have disappeared by high summer.

Much of the Dene has proved unstable in the past and there is frequent evidence of mudslides and rock falls.

The tree cover in the Dene may have been frequently coppiced during the eighteenth and nineteenth centuries, and there are introduced species such as sycamore, beech and larch, but it is still basically an ash-dominant wood with principal attendants of wych elm, oak and yew. This is the most extensive northerly occurrence of yew woodland and, as may be expected, some of the contorted forms and grappling root systems, which clamp these survivors to the cliff edges, make them spectacular individuals. An understorey of hazel, guelder rose, spindle, privet and dogwood predominates.

The trees are so dense throughout the Dene that it is quite difficult to find many good vantage points where the scale of the place can be truly appreciated. While natural woodland occupies most of the valley bottom, there are some mighty planted trees along the upper reaches, notably beech and common limes. Judging by their size some of these were probably original plantings by the first Rowland Burdon in the eighteenth century. Whether planted or garden escapees, the dreaded rhododendron has spread through much of the Dene, land-grabbing and sunlight-quenching to the detriment of all about it. Given the chance, it would eventually suppress

the whole shrub layer of the wood, making it a very monotonous place, so the wardens have a constant battle to beat it back.

Throughout the Dene 450 different types of plants have been recorded, including many ancient woodland indicator species. Some of the rarer plants here, such as fly orchid, sword-leaved helleborine and lady's-slipper, have now disappeared or are actually extinct. One wonders if the collecting zeal of our adventurous Victorian forebears put paid to some of them. Even so, it is still possible to find lily-of-the-valley (often considered as a garden plant) growing wild, as well as the strange and singular herb-paris and the spooky little bird's-nest orchid; lacking any chlorophyll, this saprophyte derives its nutrition from rotting vegetable matter on the woodland floor. Its name comes from the shape of its root system, which resembles a small bird's nest.

There are some 3,000 different insects to be found in the Dene, of which one butterfly and one moth command most notice. History relates how Captain Blomer, a keen entomologist, paid many visits during the 1820s and 1830s and achieved what so many naturalists can still only dream about, namely the discovery of a new species of moth to which he could attach his own appellation – the Blomer's rivulet. Also of some note is a small dark brown butterfly called the northern brown argus. This was previously called the Castle Eden argus, because it was once thought unique to the Dene, but several other colonies were subsequently found in northern Britain, hence the name change. Although these butterflies used to range throughout the Dene, their food plant – rock-rose – now only grows at the seaward end, where the site opens out into meadows. You need to visit in July or August to spot them on the wing.

Castle Eden Dene is a rare retreat at any time of year; contrast its peace and tranquillity in the cool shade on a summer's day with the raw energy of the crashing falls in the depths of winter. Whatever the season, Castle Eden Dene will thrill.

COED Y RHAIADR

**Thundering falls and precarious woods on the edge of the
Brecon Beacons National Park**

Coed y Rhaiadr means 'wood of the waterfalls', and this massive expanse of woodland, covering almost 2,000 acres in the southern reaches of the Brecon Beacons National Park, is one of the very best places to head for if you crave the exhilaration and excitement of wild white water surging through deep rocky clefts, set amid wooded upland scenery.

A swift glance at the Ordnance Survey map shows the wood divided by the river valleys of the Nedd and the Mellte, and simply taking the map at face value, with its grid-like repetition of conifer symbols, would lead you to think that there might be little of interest or variety here. Study the map a bit closer, and the very mention of waterfalls suddenly raises hopes that something a bit special is worth seeking out. Closer inspection still, and a few billowing broadleaved woodland symbols are discernible along the margins of the rivers.

There are several different places to park around the edges of the wood which provide a variety of routes into the main attraction of the rivers and falls. From the north there are trails through the conifer stands or a riverside walk beginning just south of the village of Ystradfellte. Here is the famous Porth yr Ogof, the biggest cave entrance in Wales, from which the River Mellte bursts into the daylight. A gentle amble alongside the rushing river is a great way to get into the spirit of the place before you arrive at the sequence of spectacular waterfalls.

Alternatively, there are a couple of paths in to the Mellte from the west, which lead you straight to the river, across bleak upland pastures. Especially after rainy weather or, as the upland streams feed the river from the distant Beacons, when snow is melting, the roar of the river builds as you walk in. Peering over the lip of the gorge, the river lies surprisingly far below, almost lost amid the luxuriant broadleaved woodland that cloaks the steep slopes. Oak and alder

are the dominant species – many trees showing signs of coppicing, but not for many a year. Some of the alders in particular sit squarely on wonderful knobbly, burry stools, covered in mosses and lichens.

Taking the sensible route along a gentle gradient, you come first to the deep, base thunder of the Sgwd Clun Gwyn – uppermost of the feature waterfalls on the Mellte. Even when the river is in full spate a huge, level slab of rock beneath the falls allows you (with care, as it can be slippery) to get the spray in your face. A bridge a little way upriver permits access to the recommended path, which leads you down to one of the most impressive of the falls. Sgwd Isaf Clun Gwyn arrives relatively quietly across another wide rock shelf, before slipping over the rim into a raging cataract which consists of two giant steps channelling into a narrow passage at the base, churning and grumbling ever downward. This remarkably damp, sheltered gorge harbours an amazing 230 species of mosses and ferns – some extremely rare. There are several other falls to be traced along the river's course, but striking off up the eastern slope of the Mellte eventually brings you breathless and elated to a high-level path. From here the views out across the wood as well as straight down into the deep gorge from which you have just emerged are extensive and rewarding.

This upland path leads to what many consider the greatest gem of the Waterfalls Walk. However, along the way some unusual features are worth noting. Below, the oak still proves dominant, but above the path dark stands of conifers hold sway; and yet here and there strange ghosts appear through the gloom: wood banks, which indicate defunct boundaries or hedges, and along them impressive outgrown coppice stools of ash, oak, hazel and beech, some clearly showing evidence of historic laying, with old boughs cut and bent horizontally.

Sgwd Isaf Clun Gwyn on the Afon Mellte on a crisp April day.

RIGHT In May the creamy clusters of rowan flowers hang high above the River Mellte in Coed y Rhaiadr.

BELOW RIGHT An old oak coppice stool adorned with lichens and mosses. What appears to be an aerial root has emerged from the hollow bole before plunging below the surrounding moss. This may have taken many years to occur, but it affirms the tree's commitment to longevity.

OPPOSITE The peaty brown waters of the River Hepste thunder over Sgwd yr Eira

Other remnants of an ancient treescape include old rowan pollards, coppiced small-leaved limes and some fine crab apples.

After crossing the promontory between the Mellte and Hepste valleys, you begin the steep descent into the latter. Again the roar of huge volumes of water in a big hurry filters up through the trees and, after losing count of the rustic steps, which zigzag down to the river, you stand before Sgwd yr Eira. The raw power of this fall is awesome and you can experience it extremely close at hand, for a rock ledge leads behind the falls, where you can stare out through the massive curtain of water. If you can brave the extreme chill of a freezing winter's day, the incredible forms of these waterfalls when frozen are a memorable sight. Caught as if in some gigantic three-dimensional filmic freeze-frame, the blue-white ice hangs, immobilized above the void.

It seems hard to believe, but expert canoeists ride the white water down these rivers, although there must be places too extreme where portage is required. Lots of outdoor pursuits organizations take climbing parties through as well, so you may come upon orange-clad kids or company managers doing the obligatory team-building weekend. This is an exciting place to visit, where you can follow narrow, sometimes precarious paths above the rocky gorges below; so, like the specialists, it's important to go well equipped and to take great care at all times.

LOVERS OF LIMESTONE

EAVES WOOD

Luxuriant life on the limestone pavement of Silverdale, at the northern tip of Lancashire

Wherever you find limestone you'll come across a fascinating array of trees and plants. From the lush, flower-strewn valleys of the Derbyshire Peak District, to the rugged clefts through the Mendips, or the spartan upland pavements of North Yorkshire, the botanical promise is infinitely rewarding. So, it's no surprise that there's an equally exciting pocket of limestone where the top end of Lancashire nudges the southern tip of Cumbria.

Silverdale and Arnside, an area designated as an Area of Outstanding Natural Beauty, contains a collection of startlingly luxuriant woods which thrive on a seemingly harsh, hard landscape of lowland limestone pavement. Unlike the similar upland pavements of Yorkshire, where much harsher weather conditions and colder temperatures restrict plants to hiding deep within the grikes (a northern term for rock clefts) and where only a few truly robust trees such as hawthorn, ash and rowan can hack it, these lowland pavements are excessively verdant, almost to the point where the stone itself is completely hidden beneath moss and undergrowth.

From the car park at Eaves Wood a single path leads you into one corner of the wood, but you are soon faced with a multitude of choices – to take a relatively gentle stroll in tune with the contours along one of the main westerly paths, or to strike off uphill into the denser undergrowth. You don't have to look far from the path as you walk in to discover one of the most special trees of Eaves Wood. Small-leaved lime has been one of Britain's core native broadleaved species for thousands of years, but its range in England is normally across the southern half of the

Ancient small-leaved lime coppice stools on the moss-covered limestone pavement in Eaves Wood. Because they are growing in this rockbound situation and were once regularly coppiced their relatively small size belies their true antiquity. These are native limes near the northern limit of their natural range in Britain.

country, in slightly warmer climes. However, in a few sheltered spots in the north it has endured, but not by regeneration from seed, as it has long been too cold for the tree to set viable seed. Its continuing presence is almost solely because of the long history of coppicing the tree. Rambling over the moss-clad limestone, equally mossy lime root systems snake this way and that. Scores of ancient coppice stools, which have been cut over for centuries, keep small-leaved lime thriving in the sheltered leeward side of Eaves Wood, nestled down safely from the nor-westers whipping in off the Irish Sea. If you leave the path to enjoy these trees at close quarters be extremely careful not to lose a leg down a half-hidden grike.

Exploring the upper reaches of the wood reveals an abundance of yews; they may be small, but in such harsh terrain they are surely extremely old. Ash, oak, rowan, hazel and beech all feature in the broadleaved cover, the latter almost certainly introduced at some period. Ash shows its pedigree as the champion

colonizer, with tiny trees springing from the most unlikely and inhospitable rock hollows. Sometimes the trees' progress has been so constricted that natural bonsai forms emerge. There is even the odd crab apple, its delicate pink blossom highlighted against the sombre yews. At the top of the wood there are a great many Scots pines – the beautiful large ruddy platelets of the bark redolent of the true natives of Scotland; so these might be vestiges of the original pine woods which retreated in the wake of the ice sheet many thousands of years back, but equally they may have been introduced using native stock. The lattice patterns of their roots cast a net across the woodland paths, and it's easy to go flying if you're not watching your step.

There are also several open glades and meadows here, where the flowers come into their own. Rarities to look out for include dark red helleborine and bloody crane's-bill, and you may be lucky enough to spot pearl-bordered fritillaries fluttering by.

ABOVE 'The Ring o' Beeches' - a mid nineteenth-century tree 'folly' in the middle of the wood.

OPPOSITE
ABOVE Morecambe Bay whitebeam is one of the rare *Sorbus* microspecies, found only within a very localised area of north-west Lancashire.

BELOW On the open ground at the top of the wood the common rock-rose makes a pretty show in early summer.

This is predominantly ancient woodland, but here and there you can trace the influence of the Victorians wreaking a little rustic management to make an accessible wilderness: paths lined out with rocks gathered from the surrounding woodland floor, a little flight of steps here, a gateway there and, at the summit of the wood, with stupendous views out across Morecambe Bay, the so-called Pepper Pot – a modest stone folly, built to commemorate Queen Victoria's Golden Jubilee in 1887. This really is a cracking place to sit and picnic with the glorious panorama of the nearby coast the perfect accompaniment to your alfresco meal. In early summer the ground is strewn with the bright yellow flowers of the pretty little rock rose.

Descending back into the wood it is easy to lose your bearings, as there are many paths zigzagging and criss-crossing everywhere. There are a few special trees to look out for, one of the rarest being the *Sorbus* microspecies *Sorbus lancastriensis*, commonly known as Morecambe Bay whitebeam – a tree only endemic to a handful of these ancient woods around Silverdale. There are only a few specimens here and the best time to spot them is in early spring, when the creamy green foliage contrasts perfectly with the surrounding dark, dense fronds of the yews. Some of the best yews are in the very heart of Eaves Wood and, although not of any great size in national terms, their precarious and austere habitat on top of the limestone probably makes them far more venerable than they might immediately appear. Such trees will be growing exceptionally slowly here. On lower ground, and probably planted in the mid-nineteenth century, is a strange circle of beech trees, unsurprisingly known as the Ring o' Beeches.

There are several wonderful woods of this type in the area, and if you only visit one other make it Gait Barrows. Set on much flatter terrain than Eaves Wood and also much more open in terms of overall tree canopy, Gait Barrows is a weird surreal landscape. This National Nature Reserve has an even more diverse range of trees, flowers, fungi (1,600 different species), butterflies and moths (800 different species) than Eaves Wood, and here you may even catch sight of a hen harrier or hear the strange booming of the bittern.

EBBOR GORGE

A densely wooded cleft in the Mendips of Somerset

View skyward from the bottom of Ebbor Gorge through the towering ash canopy.

By far the most popular haunt for visitors to the Mendip Hills of Somerset is Cheddar Gorge. Around half a million people a year visit the biggest gorge in the UK, far famed for its reputation as the home of Britain's most ubiquitous cheese, although a mere token proportion of the nation's consumption is still made here. Many approach Cheddar across the flat expanse of the Levels, virtually bereft of woodland, but tree-clad by virtue of the willows, poplars and alders which map the streams and drainage ditches. Approaching Cheddar from the north, taking the steep descent that zigzags down the gorge, the impact of towering limestone cliffs adorned with precariously rooted trees is unmissable. Cheddar Gorge is impressive, but with a yearning to avoid the traffic (and some of those half a million visitors) there are other gorges of a much more peaceful nature, yet equally exciting, to explore nearby.

In the hills above Wookey Hole lies Ebbor Gorge, a National Nature Reserve, and although not on the scale of Cheddar it is a remarkably beautiful and awe-inspiring place. The site of some 101 acres is large enough to get that feeling of isolation and adventure, particularly outside the summer season when fewer tourists venture forth. A spring morning in May or early June, when the foliage greens are still vivid and fresh and the flowers are at their very best, is always rewarding.

The main route through the reserve is of quite a strenuous nature. Rugged paths lead down from the car park into the bottom of the gorge, where towering ash trees sway gently in the breeze, far above. Ash is the dominant tree species here, but there are also plenty of wych elm, oak, beech and that great opportunist sycamore, while the understorey is made up of hazel, dogwood, spindle and hawthorn. Occasionally, hornbeam is encountered, and the strangest group is one of about a dozen trees, which

would appear to have been planted in a circle around the stream. Exactly when and by whom remains a mystery. The assumption must be that the trees were introduced, although other individual hornbeams within the woods here could well be self-sown. If the first hornbeams in this wood did manage to colonize naturally, it would make the site the most westerly known in Britain where this has happened.

Once in the very bottom of the gorge the walking begins to turn more to scrambling. Boulders, buttresses and lofty crags loom above and the dense vegetation on every side tends to be impenetrable to all but the most determined of explorers. Mosses and ferns bedeck the boulders in these shady, damp clefts, while the sinuous trunks of the trees stretch ever higher in search of sunlight. In autumn the conditions down below are ideal for a fine array of fungi.

Approaching the end of the gorge has all the appearance of careering into a solid stone wall. There seems to be no way forward until, just as retracing your steps seems inevitable, a slim crevice appears beyond and you are permitted to slide between the sheer cliff sides, scaling well-worn blocks and steps, and clambering into yet another tract of beautiful woodland. This is woodland with something of a primeval feel – huge old trees list this way and that among the moss-bound rockery, some half-fallen, others completely prone. There may be management here, but it's certainly a low-key approach, which promotes the atmosphere of a wooded wilderness.

Like the trees which seek the light, you scramble further up the wood, eventually emerging on to the top of the cliffs at a stupendous viewing point. The whole gorge stretches away below like some giant's garden, offering a bird's-eye view of the dense woodland, the trees almost masking the great gaping limestone chasm. Birdsong echoes across the void and the conversations of some invisible fellow explorers, beneath the tree canopy far below, sound uncannily close. In the distance the Somerset Levels shimmer in the haze, your bearings squared by the unmistakable mound of Glastonbury Tor. Basking in the summer sunshine there's a good chance of spotting some of the gorge's special butterflies – silver-washed and high brown fritillaries or white-letter hairstreak – lured to the flower-rich turf of the cliff tops. There are also plenty of small buckthorns and whitebeams clinging to the cliff edge; the latter easily distinguished in spring by their creamy white leaves.

The gorge has evolved over a period of about 2 million years. Streams running through the valley slowly eroded the Carboniferous limestone, seeping through cracks and causing hollows eventually to become large caves. Some 200,000 years ago, during periods of freezing and thawing, water action etched ever deeper into these subterranean caverns, eventually causing them to collapse. Some of the smaller caves and hollows, which survive to this day, have yielded bones of animals such as reindeer, cave bear, wolf and lemming, which have long been extinct in Britain. Evidence of Neolithic people, who probably hunted such animals some 5,000 years ago, has also been discovered in the caves of the gorge.

Ebbor Gorge, like many other gorge woodlands in Britain, has survived largely because of its extreme terrain. It has never been suitable for grazing livestock, the extraction of great quantities of timber was never viable, and there is little sign of large-scale quarrying for limestone – unlike other parts of the Mendips which are still being clawed away by the huge demand for stone. In fact it was traditionally managed for coppice wood, and it is these coppice cycles that have helped the gorge maintain its marvellously vibrant quality to this day.

An impressive colony of *Coprinus disseminata* fungi, along with a mini-forest of ash seedlings, have taken over a fallen tree trunk in the depths of the gorge.

RIGHT Surprising, but not too frightening, this huge cave bear woven from willow waits for you in the lower reaches of Ebbor Gorge. It was recently created by sculptor Sophie Courtiour, with help from local school children.

BELOW View down from the edge of the crags into the densely wooded gorge, where ash is the dominant tree. The Somerset Levels stretch away in the far distance.

YEWS IN THEIR HIDDEN HAUNTS

KINGLEY VALE

Ancient yews below the South Downs of Sussex

The yew is a mysterious, capricious tree, jealously guarding the secrets of its vintage, growing in unruly, freakish forms and surviving in some of the most inhospitable habitats. Most of Britain's giant yews in excess of 500 years old will be encountered within the confines of churchyards, most particularly throughout England's southern counties and along the Welsh borders, where it tends to grow freely on calcareous soils. Yew often occurs as an incidental element of woods on chalk or limestone thriving happily in the open or in the shade of broadleaved trees. Its tenacity means that it can survive in some of the most difficult situations where other trees would soon perish, so it's not unusual to find substantial trees growing from rock crevices, crags or on windswept mountain tops.

Large, close-knit groups of ancient yews in a woodland setting are something of a rarity. Only a handful of such sites exist in Britain, but surely the most spectacular yew wood in the land, and one that is widely acclaimed as the oldest and best example in Europe, is to be found at the foot of the South Downs, north-west of Chichester, near the village of West Stoke. A short walk north of the village, across neatly ploughed fields, flecked white with chalky pebbles, brings you to the dark and sombre prospect of Kingley Vale.

One of the earliest references to the yews of Kingley (Kingly or Kinglye) Bottom is to be found in the Reverend C.A. Johns's *The Forest Trees of Britain* in 1847, where he describes them as 'the most remarkable assemblage of yews in Great Britain', adding 'as to when, or by whom they were planted, or indeed whether they were planted by the hand of man at all, history is silent'. Johns found about 200 yews growing in Kingley Vale, of which 'one half of them form the dense, dark grove in the depth of the bottom'. These were the largest trees, and

he estimated their age to be in the region of 900 years. Such a date for these trees almost vindicates the popular local legend that they were planted to commemorate a great victory over Viking invaders in 859. Indeed, it is also said that some of the ancient earthworks and barrows on the hills above, known locally as the Devil's Humps, mark the graves of the Norse kings who led the invasion (although they are almost certainly far too old for such an association). The name Kingley is said to mean 'burial place of kings'. Again, history is silent.

To get the maximum effect of these atmospheric woods, try visiting on a weekday, early in the morning or late evening. Pick a wild, wuthering sort of day or perhaps one shrouded in mist or fog. The eternal yews will be there, waiting, unchanged in their dark, evergreen habit, whatever the time of year. Slip into the shadows, edging respectfully among the twisted, tortured ancients; some have fallen and grown sideways; some groan and moan as if they would abandon the struggle to survive and fall any minute. Huge arching, arachnoid boughs seem about to prise the old yew boles from the mould, wrenching them forth to shamble off to some darker, secretive lair beyond the gaze of puny mortals; and you do feel insignificant and awestruck in the presence of these trees. The oldest ones are generally thought to be about 500 years old, yet recent investigations have revealed that the natural succession of these yews may go back thousands of years.

Kingley has been a National Nature Reserve since 1952 (one of the first to be designated), but its fortunes prior to that were decidedly mixed. The Victorians were obviously quite taken with this intensely gothic landscape, but the local farmers were not so deeply attached, for around the end of the

One of the largest ancient yews in Kingley Vale.

nineteenth century many of the great old yews were grubbed out to make way for agriculture. During the Second World War army units, training nearby, found it hugely fascinating to discover how many mortar bombs were required to topple an ancient yew, as well as shattering and damaging many trees with indiscriminate rifle practice. After 1952 it seemed as if a calmer future was in store for the ancient yew forest, but then along came the great storm of October 1987. There will be other storms, other traumas, but somehow it seems inconceivable that the yews will ever succumb.

Moving through the wood, on past the ancient giants, and up the hillside on a sunny spring day, soon lifts that mood of gloom and suspense that prevails beneath the yews. Crossing the tightly cropped turf, pocked with busy rabbit activity, you may see that distinctive undulating flight of a green woodpecker or spot shy roe or fallow deer skipping nimbly back inside the woodland cover as you approach. You might be entranced by the song of the nightingale

here, and there are dormice too, but the odds of seeing them are slender. Broadleaved trees, such as field maple and hawthorn, bursting into first flush vivid green and the creamy, downy leaves of newly emerged whitebeam strike a wonderful contrast with the dark yews. Breast the top of the Downs and pause to gaze at the sweeping view beneath you. In 1830 the nineteenth-century Chichester poet Charles Crocker was moved to verse:

A thousand charms now open on the view,
O'er which enchanted roves the wonderer's eye
With ever fresh delight. In stainless blue
Immensity above extends the sky:-
Below, in richest harmony, each dye
Of varied green is blended to adorn
This solitary vale, that seems to lie
Lovely as Eden on creation's morn,
Ere nature knew decay – ere pain and grief were born.

The heavy shade of the ancient yews at Kingley Vale clearly shows that virtually nothing can grow beneath them. Many of the huge arcing boughs will eventually touch the ground, layering themselves in the process, and ensuring that if anything ever happens to the parent tree a new generation of yews has been established.

ABOVE The creamy green spring foliage of whitebeam stands out among the dark yews.

BELOW LEFT Whitebeam in flower with its distinctive pale green leaves, which feel like soft felt when they first unfurl in spring.

BELOW RIGHT A fruitful season for a female yew tree. The vivid pink aril is sweet, rather tasteless, but edible; however the seed inside is poisonous.

HAUGH AND NUPEND WOODS

Strange and secret treescapes below the Woolhope Dome of Herefordshire

Squeezing into the northern limits of the Wye Valley Area of Outstanding Natural Beauty comes a marvellous complex of Herefordshire woods that drape themselves across the limestone of the Woolhope Dome. There is a large, private, mainly conifer, plantation wood to the north, but on the west side is one of the biggest publicly accessible woods in the county. Haugh Wood, owned by the Forestry Commission, although still being planted up with conifers as recently as 2005, is now set to become a showpiece site where the optimum management of natural resources will include the restoration of damaged ecosystems – in essence a welcome return for broadleaved species and their associated habitats.

Haugh Wood, which is actually pronounced 'Hoff', first appears in a document of 1544; the

Coppiced hazel and oaks etched with early morning hoar-frost in Haugh Wood.

Common spotted orchids grow in profusion along some of the wide rides.

The Forestry Commission had acquired around two-thirds of its current 850 acres of Haugh Wood in 1925 and between 1926 and 1936 it planted a lot of larch and also beech, Douglas fir and some oak. The main remit for most of the next sixty years would be softwood production to the detriment of the native woodland, much of it ancient. Strong feelings have been expressed to this day that if the Forestry Commission had managed Haugh for its natural broadleaved trees, to produce quality hardwood from the very start, the woodland of today would not only be of far superior landscape character and biodiversity, but also more commercially profitable.

Some twenty-four years after the Forestry Commission officially recognized that broadleaved woodland should be maintained and enhanced, it is now grasping the nettle and beginning to put conservation management into action in much of this wood which is, after all, a designated Site of Special Scientific Interest. The rides and paths have been cleared and widened, with two very accessible butterfly trails laid out with informative interpretation boards along the route. You may spot rare pearl-bordered fritillaries or grizzled skippers. In late spring the drifts of common spotted orchids along the ride margins are very special and you can still seek out the rare lily-of-the-valley and herb-paris. The broadleaved trees are mainly oak, ash, field maple and wych elm, with a few native limes, and an understorey of hawthorn, blackthorn, hazel, holly and occasional spindle, wayfaring tree, wild service and yew. Haugh's biggest claim to fame is that it is currently among Britain's top ten woods for invertebrates, with some 600 species recorded. Changes for the better are washing over Haugh Wood.

Barely half a mile to the south-west, between Haugh and the village of Fownhope, lies the splendid little Nupend Wood; only 13 acres, and so a real minnow in the context of this book, yet one of Herefordshire Nature Trust's woodland gems. Nupend and adjoining West Wood and Fownhope Park Wood are quite feasibly outliers to the Haugh system, but their composition, even though much of West Wood in particular has been lost to conifers, is redolent of extremely ancient woodland. Yew features as a major element in these woods, but usually on the poorer, rockier terrain that would appear historically to have been of little use to foresters for planting or tending broadleaved species. Some huge, old, outgrown

name probably derives from 'high' ground which would have been waste or poor ground at the upper end of the parish. Haugh's early incarnation was probably as heathland with scrub, used by local communities for grazing livestock, before enclosure for woodland during the sixteenth century. Heath plants such as heather and blaeberry are still to be found there. The wood's history is fairly sketchy before the end of the seventeenth century. However, extensive research by woodland historian and ecologist David Lovelace recently uncovered a remarkable document in the Hereford Record Office. The Haugh Wood workbook is a comprehensive record of all the day-to-day working practice and commercial transactions in the wood between 1702 and 1818. It was a woodland historian's dream find, which revealed that Haugh was a classic coppice wood worked on a twenty-year cycle of annual fellings. Typically, cordwood (cut firewood: bigger than twigs, smaller than logs) was converted to charcoal for the iron industry, and tan bark was supplied to the tanners and dyers, while oak and ash standards were nurtured for timber.

Stinking iris in Nupend Wood.

small-leaved and large-leaved lime coppice stools can be found deep in the woods, as well as numerous large oak and ash coppice stools.

A good way to get straight in among the yews is to enter the bottom of Nupend Wood, just off the Fownhope to Woolhope road. A ridge of Wenlock limestone ascends steeply, through clumps of stinking iris, beneath a dense canopy of gnarled and twisted yews clinging grimly to the crest of the rocky spine. None of them is particularly large, but their precarious situation on such poor ground may well have caused them to grow extremely slowly, and so their modest size belies their antiquity. Some of the trees show evidence of coppicing in the distant past – exactly for what purpose is a mystery. Fuel wood is a possibility, but staves for longbows most unlikely. Where the yews have been left to their own devices they dominate, for little or nothing grows beneath them, but there is a sense here that just maybe yew once covered a lot more of this wood, before foresters favoured the oak and ash. The tangled webs of the yews' roots are a continual fascination, criss-crossing or fusing with each other, grasping and encapsulating limestone pebbles and rocky outcrops. Hundreds of incredible old yews may be discovered throughout Nupend and West Woods; every single one a distinct and unique character.

The lower levels of Nupend are floristically the richest areas, around two long-abandoned quarries, where the yews give way to undulating grassland and a wealth of lime-loving plants such as ploughman's-spikenard, greater butterfly orchid, pyramidal orchid, marjoram, yellow-wort and yet more stinking iris – an unfortunate epithet for a handsome plant, so called because the leaves, when rubbed, smell of stale, raw beef. As expected, this woodland flower meadow is a great haunt for butterflies; grizzled skipper, marbled white and silver-washed fritillary all regular visitors. You may sometimes find adders basking on the sunny banks, so have a care where you sit.

In early winter flocks of redwings and fieldfares visit the wood to binge on the abundant yew berries. Marsh tit, chiffchaff, nuthatch and both green and great spotted woodpeckers are all to be found here too. A most startling experience, while taking a photograph of the yews, was a brush with an extremely large tawny owl, that must have been watching me at work for some time before it dropped silently from its branch, no more than 20 feet from me, and coasted lazily off to a more private corner of the wood, to continue its daytime nap. It was a little spooky, but amazing all at once – I felt buoyed by the moment for the rest of the day.

After a rain storm the fabulous colours of the yew's bark are revealed in Nupend Wood.

LIMES THAT REFUSE TO LIE DOWN

BARDNEY LIME WOODS

The formidable force of lime coppice in Lincolnshire

A look at the map shows that Lincolnshire is one of lowland Britain's most sparsely wooded counties, and a drive across it confirms this picture. Even field trees and hedgerow trees seem somewhat thinner on the ground too. Typically, many of the boundaries are long straight hawthorn hedges of the enclosure period, partitioning the massive fields of arable agriculture. Because the land is so very flat, hardly ever rising higher than 500 feet, it is difficult to appreciate the woods that are out there. Although there are almost 7,000 acres of woodland, less than a quarter is considered to be of ancient origin, and in a county the size of Lincolnshire that's not a lot: about 0.33 per cent of the landmass, to be exact.

The twentieth century saw relatively little woodland clearance compared to the previous hundred years, yet a different threat was posed to what few ancient woods still survived. The Forestry Commission, which purchased a large group of broadleaf woods to the east of Lincoln in 1945, planted ranks of conifers, as well as some oak, throughout the mid-twentieth century. This was before anyone had really thought about the conservation aspects of these very special native woods and so, until relatively recent times, the main thrust of forestry practice was aimed at high-volume softwood timber production. This could so easily have seen the suppression and disappearance of the most remarkable feature of this group of nine woods, located between the villages of Wragby and Bardney – the dominant presence of small-leaved lime.

The Lincolnshire Limewoods Project was set up in 1997; jointly funded by the Forestry Commission, in association with Lincolnshire County Council, Natural England and Lincolnshire Wildlife Trust, it is an innovation with three basic aims – to promote access, education and enjoyment and heritage management. In fact the whole area covered by these woods is designated as the Bardney Limewoods National Nature Reserve. It is small-leaved lime which marks these woods out as something special; they are in fact the greatest concentration of lime-dominant woods anywhere in Britain. The botanist and conservationist Peter Marren points out that the prevalence of *lin* and *bass* place names in Lincolnshire suggests that the tree was once much more widespread in the past. *Bass* refers to the fibrous underbark or bast of the lime, which was once used to weave a coarse fabric and for rope making. Pollen records from post-glacial deposits in peat beds and fossil remains of lime-specific bark beetles also confirm a past predominance of lime in eastern England.

Superficially most of these woods might appear to be rather monotonous conifer stands with a few broadleaf stands tucked in between, but like a sleeping giant the true original nature of these woods lies just below the surface. Recent conservation management is now giving the broadleaf cover chance to reawaken and be a major element once again. From the outset this seems unlikely territory for lime, as elsewhere in Britain it shows a preference for calcareous soils, but here it thrives on neutral, even acidic soils. The natural mixture is usually small-leaved lime, ash, oak, birch and hazel. As ever, alder and willow find purchase in the damper areas.

The biggest of these woods, Chambers Farm Wood, is actually an agglomeration of four smaller woods – Minting Wood, Hatton Wood, Ivy Wood and Little Scrubbs Wood – all interconnected and well served with a network of paths and broad rides. Take a couple of steps off the path to look inside the broadleaf wood and you're invariably surrounded by lime coppice stools – some are huge outgrown stools with massive poles, which may have gone fifty to a hundred years since they were last cut, while

Small-leaved lime regenerating from root suckers in Chambers Farm Wood. The predominance of the species in these woods is clearly illustrated by the carpet of lime leaves.

most others have been cut over more recently. The gnarled bases to these stools suggest great antiquity. Some trees have arched over, touched the ground and layered themselves; some have multiplied as great clumps of root suckers.

Next to Little Scrubbs Wood a recent change to stimulate biodiversity in the heart of the woodland complex has been the creation of Little Scrubbs Meadow to provide a range of flowers, grasses and sedges to encourage rare butterflies such as dingy skipper and marsh fritillary. Sheep are grazed here between May and September and a late cut of hay is often taken. A walk over the meadow in autumn reveals several tree species already trying their utmost to turn this open ground back into woodland, with oak, willow and birch seedlings aplenty and, here and there, deep red rashes of guelder rose leaves. Although many of these will have to be cut back if it is to remain an open space, it would be fascinating to see how quickly the meadow returned to closed-cover woodland if left as an area of non-intervention.

Some of the special birds worth watching out for include chiffchaff, blackcap, willow warbler, nightingale, whitethroat, goldcrest and all three native woodpeckers. On June evenings this is also a place to come and find glow worms.

A couple of miles west of Chambers Farm lies another of the Bardney lime woods with a slightly different character. College Wood again appears to be strung about a regular grid pattern of forestry tracks, the pines, spruces and hemlocks in resolute blocks. There are also some large compartments of beech. However, it seems that the Forestry Commission indulged in a little experimentation here a few years back and small stands of southern beech and red oak, quite a stunner in autumn, greet you near the main entrance. Oak, ash and birch are here, as well as plenty of aspen, but it is the small-leaved lime that bursts forth from between and beneath the sombre conifer boughs. These are trees that refuse to lie down. Closer inspection reveals many outgrown coppiced limes reaching for the light. Even inside the wood, wherever there's a patch of light squeezing in the limes are there – often only arising as spindly little saplings regenerating from ancient root systems. There are reports, though, of lime seedlings having been found in College Wood – a very exciting development if this is really so, and a positive response indeed to global warming.

ABOVE It wasn't just conifers that were planted on top of so many of the Bardney lime woods. The autumnal colours of red oaks, planted some years ago in College Wood by the Forestry Commission, make a pretty good show.

RIGHT An 8-foot-wide small-leaved lime coppice stool resembles a small hedge. Since few of the individual stems are of any great size it may come as a surprise to know that a tree of this size could well be many hundreds of years old.

This small-leaved lime stool
is thought to be the largest
in Chambers Farm Wood, and
it is certainly many a year
since it was last coppiced.

WYE VALLEY

**Emerging from the gloom or forgotten in the landscape,
huge old limes still thrive in the Welsh borders**

To say that any of the woods of the Wye Valley are predominantly lime might be stretching a point, but it's certainly within reason to believe that many of them were once lime dominant before climate changes that began some 5,000 years ago saw the native limes begin to draw back their range in the lowland broadleaved woodlands of Britain. Cooler, wetter conditions simply weren't conducive for the limes to set viable seed and this, coupled with their sensitivity to grazing (most animals relish lime leaves), saw a gradual decline in natural regeneration.

The serpentine valley of the Wye between Ross-on-Wye and Chepstow has long been a popular destination for tourists, coming to prominence in the late eighteenth century when the opinionated aesthete, scholar and artist William Gilpin first published an account of his tour. It was Gilpin who coined the term 'picturesque', said to be derived

LEFT View down into the Wye Valley from the Offa's Dyke Path above Shorn Cliff, with Tintern Abbey far below.

OPPOSITE The massive hollow base of a veteran lime pollard in Church Grove. After some of the conifers which were crowded around it were removed, and sunlight flooded in once again, the signs of recovery are clearly evident.

The distinctive heart-shaped (cordate) leaves of small-leaved lime.

from the Italian *pittoresco*, meaning 'after the manner of painters', whereby every aspect of the landscape became an elemental contributor, judged for its aesthetic merits as part of some perfectly perceived, idyllic composition. Gilpin's outpourings not only appealed to the affluent classes who could afford the luxury of travel and the diversion of art, but also sparked a new direction for landowners and landscapers, most notably Uvedale Price at Foxley and Richard Payne Knight at Downton.

Beneath the veneer of Gilpin's picturesque lay a working valley where the common folk toiled to make a living – an incidental element, as far as Gilpin was concerned, which he found rather quaint and conveniently in keeping with his overall impressions. The Industrial Revolution was under way; ironically it most likely lined the pockets of many of the tourists who flocked to the Wye, and yet it was the labourers and artisans at the bottom of the social scale who fired industry. Coal was mined in the adjacent Forest of Dean, iron ore was extracted from the hills above the valley and coppice wood for charcoal and tan bark were cut from the woods. A walk today through much of the lower Wye woodland reveals innumerable charcoal hearths as small platforms or ledges set into the hillsides, with an abundance of long-outgrown coppice stools close by. Scrape away

a little of the leafy loam and tiny scraps of charcoal still lie just beneath the surface.

The role of broadleaved trees in the valley's working woodland had changed by the end of the nineteenth century. What had been an intensively managed landscape of coppice stands and wood pastures, with attendant pollards, became semi-redundant. Some trees were still cut for fuel wood, but overall the early twentieth century saw a period of neglect and abandonment, followed by the instigation of a new regime introducing large plantations of coniferous trees. Usually this was at the expense of the broadleaved trees, which were either grubbed out or overplanted so that the eventual loss of sunlight killed them. Remarkably, though, many trees survived this treatment, and some of the most tenacious were the native limes.

Along a large tract of the eastern slopes, south of Redbrook, conifers have dominated Cadora Woods for the last forty years or more, but this is all set to change. The Woodland Trust has acquired Cadora and discovered many of the ancient broadleaved trees have managed to survive beneath the conifers. Oak, ash, beech and some stupendous small-leaved lime coppice stools, as well as a few ancient pollards, released from their gloom, are slowly gathering strength and regenerating.

How on earth this veteran lime pollard has managed to hang in there is nothing short of a miracle. Hemmed in for several decades by ranks of conifers, hollowed out and only grasping the hillside with the aid of aerial roots, it will be fascinating to see how long it can survive now that the Woodland Trust has given it a helping hand.

Both species of native limes – the small-leaved and its scarcer cousin the large-leaved – are found in the Wye Valley woods. Identifying the two different trees can be tricky, but close examination of the distinctive heart-shaped leaves distinguishes one from the other. The small-leaved lime, as the name suggests, usually has the smaller leaves – anywhere from just over half an inch to 3 inches long, decidedly glossy on top and bearing distinctive tufts of orange-brown hairs around the leaf veins on the undersides. Large-leaved lime usually bears leaves 4 to 6 inches long, which are also slightly hairy on both sides, more so underneath.

The section of the valley below Monmouth delivers the richest pickings, but the limes occur in some number all the way up to Hereford. They are secretive trees for the most part, usually tucked away beneath the canopy rather than out in the open. Inevitably they bear the signs of human management: coppice stools, sometimes 6 to 8 feet across, with massive outgrown poles, which have probably not been cut for well over a century. Such stools are usually found within the woods, but as you walk the route of the Offa's Dyke Path you'll discover numerous old stools in hedgerows around pastures, which have now achieved the splendid, domed proportions of high-forest trees (albeit with multiple stems).

Maybe these are woodland trees that date back to a time before the fields were carved out of the wood. Around areas of defunct wood pasture or along old boundary banks ancient pollards with gigantic, burry pantomime tree boles stand sentinel. For centuries these ancient limes have largely survived by dint of human activity or by reproducing through layering and suckering. Sometimes a tree is blown down, yet limes often manage to hang on with barely a handful of roots still in the ground. An old tree, once prone, may throw up a host of new stems along the length of the old bole, forming its own lime 'hedge'.

Lime hunting is great fun in the Wye Valley, but the whole area has so much more to offer the tree and woodland enthusiast. Seek out some rare whitebeam microspecies, discover a mysterious grove of ancient sweet chestnut pollards, and be amazed by some remarkable old yew trees hanging on in truly precarious situations. There are magnificent vistas across and along the river to be enjoyed from numerous high vantage points – Tintern Abbey from Shorn Cliff; Chepstow and its castle from the Piercefield Walks; the classic meander loop at Lancaut, viewed from Wyndcliff, summoning memories of O level geography lessons … not quite the oxbow lake yet, though.

WORKING WOODLAND

BRADFIELD WOODS

Over 750 years of continuous woodland management in the heart of Suffolk

Peter Fordham is a happy man. For twenty-eight years he's been looking after one of Britain's most vibrant woods; a very special place with a working pedigree stretching back for hundreds of years. A walk through Bradfield with Peter opens up a treasure chest of biodiversity and woodmanship reflecting the past, but also very much the present status of this splendid woodland.

Peter has overseen many coppice fellings here, with most compartments cut on a 25-year cycle. He enthuses about the regeneration, not just of the trees, but also the ground flora and the attendant butterflies and birdlife, which regular management encourages. Remembering the early years, he laughs, recalling the many visitors who were concerned by what they saw as wholesale destruction going on. Then, reassurance was required, but now almost everyone seems to be comfortable with the whole idea of what coppicing means to the woods. It allows the sunlight to flood the woodland floor once again and this, along with the maintenance of the paths and rides, is what encourages Bradfield's plants and wildlife. Apparently, more than 370 different species of flowering plants along with forty-two types of native trees and shrubs have been recorded here. Part of the reason for this is the great variety of growing conditions – not just light and shade, but also dry and damp areas and a variety of soil types.

Bradfield Woods, close to the village of Felsham, south-east of Bury St Edmunds, can trace an unbroken history of management back to the mid-thirteenth century – 1252, to be exact. The two woods were then recorded as Munces Park (an Anglo-Saxon spelling of Monk's Park), and Felshamhall Wood which, as landscape historian and scholar Oliver Rackham tells us, derives from the Old English *Ffelshamhalle*, meaning the 'wood at the Felsham corner' of the Bradfield St George parish.

The ancient history of Bradfield Woods is still boldly drawn in the landscape. Felshamhall Wood is surrounded by an impressive wood bank. Such a demarcation line indicated the property of the monks of the abbey of Bury St Edmunds, but, more importantly, this indispensable man-made structure kept marauding herbivores such as deer, cattle and sheep out of the woods. The absence of such animals gave the newly coppiced trees a chance to regenerate without having the new growth regularly browsed off. Today, it's difficult to exclude deer, but after a compartment has been coppiced a dead hedge made up from the brash helps to protect the stools. By the time these barriers have naturally broken down, after two or three years, the new coppice growth should be strong enough to withstand the deer's attention. Because trees that grew along the banks could well have been accessible to animals in adjoining pastures, they were traditionally pollarded, so that by cutting poles at a height of about 8 feet they were always beyond their reach. Most of the surviving pollards seem to be oaks. The presence of a handful of oak pollards dotted throughout the woods indicates that the regime here has varied slightly over the years. These are usually strange, gnarled old trees with little obvious useful timber in them, often growing on sand lenses (small depressions of a predominantly sandy soil). Life was tough for these oldsters and it seems that they were caught between two stools; never growing into valuable timber trees, yet becoming more than mere coppice. Perhaps their strange angular boughs were sought after for knees and ribs for shipbuilding.

The adjoining Monk's Park does not immediately betray its original role for this was once a deer park. A map of 1700 clearly shows the wood, then more than double its current size, with clearings marked as meadows, which Rackham believes were medieval

Peter Fordham trimming hazel rods that will be bundled up and sold as bean sticks. This compartment of Bradfield Woods has just been coppiced once again after 25 years, leaving a few standards of oak and ash to mature further.

launds (where deer could graze). The word lawn is derived from laund – meaning an area of grassland with few, if any, trees. Any banks along the original edge of this wood were meant to keep deer in rather than out. The structure of the wood today seems little different from Felshamhall Wood to the casual observer, but the feature known as Hewitt's Field is the last surviving meadow or laund of the old deer park. To think that more than half of Monk's Park had been grubbed out prior to 1969 seems sad, if nor verging on tragic.

At the point where the two Bradfield Woods abut there is a pond. Vaguely crescent or fish shaped, it has attracted the latter appellation. Fish Pond, which is fed by underground springs, would have provided water for the thirsty deer in the park, while also forming a natural boundary to stop them entering Felshamhall Wood. Equally, it's not beyond the bounds of possibility that it was once stocked with

fish to service the local manors, thus giving rise to the name. Keep an eye out for kingfishers here.

In the past the coppice produce was used for many different purposes. In 1926 Fitzrandolph and Hay, in a survey entitled *The Rural Industries of England & Wales*, remarked that in Suffolk 'hurdle-makers are found here in the villages within a few miles of one another, as at Welnetham, Bradfield St George and Bradfield St Clare. The close folding of sheep on the arable land creates a demand for hurdles in considerable quantities.' The hurdle-makers, using large amounts of hazel, also made broaches (twisted wood staples) and thatch pegs of hazel or sometimes of ash, clothes-props, pea-sticks and birch brooms or besoms.

The demand for all these products has so diminished that few people can make a sustainable living from such things today. Currently, Bradfield's coppice wood is largely sold for two purposes. The

A different compartment in Bradfield Woods, photographed in 1996, shows healthy regrowth after only one year since coppicing. You can see the dead hedge protecting the compartment in the lower left hand corner.

During my visit in 2008 I discovered that this view had completely disappeared – 12 years of regeneration can make a great difference to the view.

LEFT A clump of oxlips, a regional speciality of ancient woods in Cambridgeshire and Suffolk, springs anew through a gap in a pile of poles, left in a recently coppiced area. These flowers respond particularly well after coppicing, but they are a favourite titbit for deer, so fencing off compartments is essential.

RIGHT Wood anemones confirm the ancient status of the woods. Windflower seems a perfect alternative name for these delicate little flowers, which flutter with only the slightest of breezes.

thinner poles are bundled and bought by many of the locals for bean- and pea-sticks – an important way of adding value to British woods and reducing the carbon footprint made by importing masses of bamboo from across the globe. Larger poles, principally ash, are logged for sale as firewood – an aspect of sales currently on a steep increase as people turn away from the frightening price of oil and look to woodburners to heat their homes.

After the local populace witnessed the loss of Monk's Park in the 1960s, a concerted effort was made to save what was left, and in 1970 Suffolk Wildlife Trust managed to purchase Bradfield Woods, which in 1994 became a National Nature Reserve. The history may be fascinating, but you don't need to know all this simply to walk among the trees

with all your senses on alert; listening out for the melodious song of the nightingale; keeping your eyes peeled for the twenty-four species of butterflies, four different kinds of deer (roe, red, fallow and muntjac), badgers or the rare dormouse; transported by the heady scent of honeysuckle or bluebells.

WYRE FOREST

A last vestige of the tan bark industry alongside modern forestry in Worcestershire

The bucolic nature of so much of Britain's wooded forests, particularly those tracts which still remain dominated by broadleaved trees, makes it difficult to imagine that they have had a complex history driven for many centuries by industry and the local economy. In England and Wales there are many forests of continuous conifers – tree farms or timber factories by any other names – and yet these relatively modern plantations do have wildlife and amenity value. Some of our most familiar forests, such as the New Forest, Sherwood, Savernake or the Forest of Dean, are a diverse mosaic of broadleaves and conifers. The Wyre Forest is no exception.

The Wyre Forest today amounts to about 6,000 acres on the western side of the River Severn, near Bewdley in Worcestershire, although the northern part is actually in Shropshire – the Dowles Brook, the main watercourse through the forest, constitutes the county boundary. It is said that the name Wyre derives from a Celtic tribe called the Weorgoran; the name further adopted by the Romans for their settlement of Wyreceaster – today's city of Worcester.

The modern economy of the Wyre Forest is largely in the hands of the Forestry Commission, which acquired almost half of the total forest area in 1928 when, in the aftermath of the First World War, there was a huge national effort to grow a lot more of our own softwood trees; so that in the event of another conflict and drastically reduced levels of imports Britain would not be starved of timber. To this effect the Commission set about planting massed ranks of conifers, principally Douglas fir and larch, but also spruces, pines, cypress and western red cedar. It also planted a great deal of beech. With the best intentions for the nation's timber self-sufficiency, these plantations drastically altered much of the character of the forest – ancient working woodland that had evolved over many centuries.

Until the arrival of the conifers, the Wyre was an area of broadleaved woodland dominated by oak – usually sessile on the more acidic, drier soils of hilltops and steep valley sides with the pedunculate favouring the damper, alkaline alluvial soils of the valley bottoms. Historically, most of this oak cover was coppiced on a regular basis, both for charcoal burning and for bark peeling; although records show that to obtain the very best-quality charcoal the burners of the Wyre actually preferred to use holly or beech – both locally abundant. On the other hand, oak was indispensable for the bark peelers. Oak has the highest content of tannic acid in the bark; the fundamental requirement for the leather tanneries, where all the bark was bound. A vibrant industry thrived on the banks of the Severn at Bewdley, due to a plentiful supply of water and bark and an excellent waterway for transporting the finished leather out to the waiting world. With the introduction of chemical substitutes for bark tannin

A bright winter's day among oak coppice in the Wyre Forest.

A close-up view of the barking iron, which is used to lever off the oak bark. The bark releases better during the springtime when the sap is rising.

in the early twentieth century bark peeling virtually ceased, and by 1928 the last of Bewdley's tanneries had closed down.

There are several detailed accounts of the gangs of coppicers and peelers who worked the woods of the Wyre in the nineteenth century. Traditionally, the peeling season began on 24 April, when the sap was rising, thus making it easier to separate the bark from the poles. Gangs of men and women (and even young children) decamped to the woods for up to six weeks to peel bark. The men cut the poles, the women peeled with the distinctive barking irons, and as often as not the children scurried back and forth stacking the peeled bark.

On a token scale, compared to the boom years of the eighteenth and nineteenth centuries, bark peeling continues in the Wyre Forest today. Paul Jackson, who runs a business called Coppice Creations, working with his father and his son, has a small annual contract with a Cornish tannery that still prefers to use traditional oak bark for tanning its leather – believing that it makes a superior-quality product. Paul negotiates with the Forestry Commission to coppice small compartments of oak for the purpose. The poles are cut and taken back to the yard for peeling. The method of peeling is exactly the same as it always was, using identical hand tools. Paul uses the stripped poles, known as black poles, to make rustic furniture, garden arches and fence panels. He also uses a lot of coppiced sweet chestnut for such purposes too, but this bark is of no use to the tanners.

In much the same way as in the past, the ongoing coppicing of the woodland is good for both this specialist niche in the local rural economy as well as helping biodiversity. Periodic coppicing and selective thinning or felling of the stands allows the regeneration of ground flora and the shrub layer and all the associated benefits for mammals, birds and invertebrates.

The broadleaved trees of the Wyre are now principally oak with beech and sweet chestnut. Ash does well on some of the occasional limestone areas, and alder dominates many of the wetter parts near the Dowles Brook and its contributory streams. Wild cherry and aspen may be encountered as well as the odd small-leaved lime or wild service tree. Hazel, hawthorn or holly tend to predominate in the understorey.

However, the real tree gem of the forest is the renowned Whitty pear – more properly the true service tree – which, with leaves like those of rowan, only larger, and fruit akin to very small pears, is a

ABOVE LEFT An 1859 engraving shows a large group, including women and children, at work removing bark from a large felled oak tree.

ABOVE The Whitty pear or true service tree which was planted in the Wyre Forest in 1913 to replace another such tree which was lost in 1862 when it was burnt down by a vandal. An extremely rare tree in the wild, its native status is currently very much under debate, and how the original tree came to be in the forest has never been explained.

member of the *Sorbus* tribe. First recorded in 1678, this single specimen had a long and colourful history, finally succumbing to the vengeful attentions of a vandal in 1862 – a miscreant who had been convicted of poaching by a local JP, knew of his affection for the tree and took revenge by way of burning it down. Fortunately, cuttings had previously been taken and planted at nearby Arley Castle. Eventually, a cutting from one of these would in turn be planted out in the middle of the forest in 1913, near the location of the original tree. It survives to this day – yet it is still a mystery as to how the original Whitty pear came to be in the forest. Some believe it to be a native, as other true service trees have recently been discovered on the south coast of Wales. Other authorities consider it an introduction from Europe, where it is relatively common.

Visiting the Wyre Forest today is a great family day out, whether you're walking the marvellous network of paths or cycling the numerous well-maintained trails. The Forestry Commission has managed to get the best out of this vast tract of woodland, both in terms of public amenity – emanating from its pivotal visitor centre at Callow Hill – and implementing a management regime for commercial forestry with due sensitivity to conservation issues.

Illustrating perfectly what the Wyre Forest was all about for hundreds of years, namely oak coppice, this healthy stool of regenerating stems keeps the traditional management alive and well.

ROMAN ROOTS

DENGE WOOD

A classic Kentish coppice wood of sweet chestnut and hornbeam

In many of the woods of East Sussex and Kent the signature tree must surely be the sweet or Spanish chestnut – not a native, it is generally thought that it was introduced by the Romans, but it is certainly extremely well naturalized in this corner of Britain. Around the city of Canterbury there is a large network of woods known as the Blean; 7,000 acres, renowned for their great swathes of sweet chestnut coppice, much of which is still regularly cut over today. The Blean is particularly well documented historically and equally well served in its present-day conservation by a conscientious band of organizations and communities.

A little removed from this woodland system, although very much in the same mould, some 5 or 6 miles south-west of Canterbury, lies Denge Wood which, in total, amounts to a little over 1,000 acres. Ownership is divided between private landowners, the Forestry Commission and the Woodland Trust, but all are pulling in the same direction – productive woodland working sympathetically with conservation.

Penny Pot Lane is the quaint name of the winding country road which leads you through the middle of Denge Wood and there are several points of access with spaces for car parking. From the outset the overriding impression is that of a dense woodland of sweet chestnut, a host of coppice stools stretching away on either side. There is a long history of planting chestnut in Kentish woods, with the usual management by coppicing, since there was never a high demand for the large-scale timber derived from mature standard trees. With its twisting grain and predilection to shakes (splitting), chestnut timber has always been of little use for construction purposes. Conversely, until about twenty years ago there was a buoyant market for chestnut coppice wood. Sweet

chestnut has the capacity to grow much faster than oak and it also quickly forms a larger zone of durable heartwood, making it ideally suited for outdoor uses. Thousands of large poles were once used by hop growers to support the wires for hop bines. Many smaller poles were cleft into palings (locally known as spiles), wired together, and used for chestnut fencing. A great deal of chestnut was also pulped for making paper. In recent times these markets have dwindled; hop production reduced due to imports and wire fencing replacing palings.

First impressions on entering Denge Wood may be rather underwhelming, as the chestnut monoculture provides little obvious variety, but delving deeper prompts the discovery of some of the wood's different and much older denizens. It soon becomes apparent that hornbeam is a major element, but in two quite distinct manifestations. From the northern end of a wide ride, which traverses the wood from north to south, a row of weird little high-cut hornbeam coppice stools, or maybe mini pollards barely 4 feet high, like strange beings with gyrating tentacles flailing skyward, march in a long line through the depths of the wood; their purpose a mystery. Perhaps they indicate a long-forgotten boundary, or maybe they were once laid into a hedge. Close by, normal ground-level cut coppice stools prevail. Evidence of boundaries can be detected within the wood as old wood banks and occasionally you come across stone markers and strategically placed yew trees. On the hedge line at the top of the wood some truly remarkable hornbeams have most definitely been laid. Marvellous forms, like giant espaliers, grow horizontally – one amazing example with outstretched limbs that have dipped to the ground, layered themselves and carried on, creating a span of more than 35 feet. From the inside looking

At the edge of Denge Wood through a huge old sweet chestnut coppice stool. More than 8 feet across, it will have been cut over for hundreds of years, but is still in good shape.

A mysterious row of high cut hornbeam coppice stools, which may have marked out a long forgotten boundary, stand in the bottom of Denge Wood. They impart a strange sense of totems belonging to some lost tribe.

out the human influence on the structure of these trees is clearly visible. From the outside looking in they present as a beautiful dense hedge – a perfect illustration why garden designers value hornbeam.

Some of the sweet chestnut coppice stools near the outer edge of the wood appear to be extremely old, with diameters of 8 to 10 feet across not unusual and many of the outgrown coppice poles soaring high into the canopy. Sycamore has done well in parts of the wood too, and has been here for some time, as some old stools attest. Oak, beech and ash also play their part and hazel and holly make up most of the understorey.

The flora of Denge confirms its status as an ancient woodland, with plenty of wood anemones and dog's mercury. The bluebells are also stupendous in spring. There is an impressive array of orchids to be found here; early-purple, fly, lesser butterfly, lady and bird's-nest orchids in the woods and twayblade, common spotted, pyramidal, greater butterfly, man and fragrant orchids on the adjacent chalk grassland.

There have been twenty-seven different types of butterflies recorded here, rarities including the green hairstreak, grizzled skipper, dingy skipper and the Duke of Burgundy fritillary. Numbers of

the latter species were in serious decline until recent years, largely due to the cessation of coppicing, for this is a butterfly which thrives along the sheltered margins and rides of these Kentish woods, as well as requiring open meadows, its food plants being primrose and cowslip. With the resumption of a coppicing regime, to open up rides and clearings, along with the close proximity of the Warren – chalk grassland, rich in flowers – the various elements which suit the Duke of Burgundy have been resurrected and now two very successful colonies thrive here – although this is the only known place in Kent that you will find this butterfly.

On a balmy day in early September the silence in the wood was almost unnerving, but there is plenty of wildlife present. Both fallow and roe deer are occasionally seen, there are some large and active badger setts, dormice are here, but secretive and, if you are lucky, you'll catch the song of the nightingale. The busiest activity that I found was the monstrous mounds of the wood ant colonies, of which there are many. As a benevolent onlooker, fascinated by these micro-worlds of organization and cooperation, I might have stayed longer, had not my potential predatorial threat required a couple of watchful sentries to give my ankles a sharp nip.

The Duke of Burgundy fritillary has benefitted greatly from renewed coppicing in the wood.

The floor of sweet chestnut woods in autumn is littered with the spiny cases of the mahogany coloured chestnuts. When the Romans first arrived in Britain and planted these trees the nuts were gathered and roasted or ground into flour. Today, neglected by man in preference for larger, imported nuts, they provide nourishment to help woodland mammals through the winter.

STOUR WOOD

Impressive sweet chestnut coppice along the Stour Estuary of Essex

Set on the south side of the Stour Estuary in Essex is a wood which offers so much, and it's not just the trees. Stour Wood is an ancient coppiced sweet chestnut woodland, with great flowers, a particularly rare butterfly and, close by, a whole host of wonderful birds to study.

Currently, Stour Wood belongs to the Woodland Trust, but is managed under an agreement with the RSPB as part of its Stour Estuary nature reserve. Historically, the management regime here has long been coppice with standards. Most of the sweet chestnut has been coppiced for hundreds of years, and there are records of this dating from 1675. Some authorities believe that the lineage of this chestnut wood may stretch back to the dawn of the species' arrival in Britain with the Roman occupation. Certainly the immense size of some of the coppice stools, often 8 or 9 feet across, imparts a strong sense of antiquity.

A walk through the wood in early spring reveals the benefits of continued coppicing to the vibrant ground flora. The extensive green and white drifts of delicate wood anemones fluttering in the soft breeze are as magnificent a show as you could find anywhere in Britain, but these are one of the flowers here that are less affected by the vicissitudes of the coppicing, simply because they bloom so early that there are few leaves on the trees to blot out the sunlight. An interesting, recent study by Mason and MacDonald, entitled *Responses of ground flora to coppice management in an English woodland* (a survey conducted between 1986 and 1997 in Stour Wood), showed conclusively how wild flowers respond to the penetration of sunlight on to the woodland floor. Most species peaked in the second and third years after a compartment was coppiced, declined rapidly until the fifth year, and after eleven years less than a third of them were

still producing flowers. Some species will produce leaves only, but others disappear altogether. It all sounds a bit serious and technical, but it makes an important point about how coppicing improves the biodiversity of the woodland. It's all a chain reaction. Introduce light; encourage the flowers; create a vibrant shrub layer; attract the butterflies; increase variety of invertebrates; influx of birdlife.

The sweet chestnut is by far the dominant species here, and the coppice stools, which are usually cut on a twenty-year rotation, are impressive; not just the huge veterans, but also the recently cut stools where twenty or thirty new stems bolt skywards. The stools are cut mainly for conservation reasons today, but there was once a large sawmill adjoining both the wood and the nearby railway line, which converted the cut poles into miles of chestnut palings, before sending them all over the country. Some wood is currently sold for firewood, some is used for construction purposes around the reserve, and some will be left on the wood floor as dead-wood habitat.

Perhaps the most important beneficiary of the coppicing is the white admiral; Stour Wood being the main site in Essex where this rare butterfly is found. Like many other rare species of British butterflies it requires very particular types of habitat to thrive; namely open sunny glades and rides, rich with flowers, where the adults can feed and bask, but also the shade of large trees with an abundance of honeysuckle where eggs can be laid and the larvae hatch and feed on this specific food plant. In many other woods honeysuckle is often treated with some disdain – a rambling strangler and mutilator of young trees. Here every effort is made to preserve the plant, even if it means a little delicate and deft handling of the chainsaw is occasionally called for during coppice works. There are some areas of the wood which are

A carpet of wood anemones spreads into the distance among the sweet chestnut coppice stools which dominate Stour Wood.

LEFT Down, but not out! A storm-blown sweet chestnut trunk lies prone on the woodland floor. Left initially as dead-wood habitat, the tree has sprung back to life, either from a few surviving roots on the stump end or from broken boughs which have dug into the earth and produced new roots.

BELOW Strange oaks along a boundary bank appear to be standing up on stilts, because the earth beneath them has eroded over many years.

so well endowed with the plant that an evening stroll may prove intoxicating: honeysuckle smells far stronger at night as it needs to attract night-flying moths which are its pollinators.

A particularly apposite snippet came to light in the late Roger Deakin's excellent book *Wildwood: A Journey Through Trees*. One night he is out moth-hunting with friends in Essex and conversation turns to a recent jaunt in Stour Wood in June, where several members of the Essex Moth Group had recorded 260 different species in one night. A remarkable tally indeed, and almost certainly contributed to by the allure of the honeysuckle.

As well as the chestnuts, Stour Wood boasts a goodly selection of other broadleaved trees, with plenty of oak, small-leaved lime, field maple, hornbeam, birch, aspen and the occasional wild service tree. Hazel is the main species of the understorey. Some of the old oaks on the boundary banks are especially worth seeking out, their odd stilt-like roots, that must once have wrapped around an earth bank, now grasp nothing, and appear to bear the trees on tiptoe above the hollows beneath.

Although the wood is stunning, and you will have every chance of observing a busy round of avian activity as you ramble and, with luck, be enraptured by the sweet song of the nightingale in spring, for all ardent birders it is the seaward side that they make for. Here the wood adjoins the salt marsh and mudflats of the Stour Estuary, famed in springtime for its black-tailed godwits, resting and feeding en route to their breeding grounds in Iceland; but perhaps more so for its nationally and internationally important counts of overwintering species of wildfowl and waders, such as Brent goose, knot, pintail, ringed and grey plover, redshank and dunlin.

Honeysuckle is an important plant for butterflies and moths in Stour Wood.

WHERE TOWN MEETS COUNTRY

EPPING FOREST

Loved by Londoners, saved for the nation, the ultimate urban–fringe woodland

Surely the supreme example of historic woodland on the urban fringe must be Epping Forest. Sitting squarely in the county of Essex, it is considered by most people to be one of London's great open spaces; it is in fact the largest, approaching 5,700 acres of which two-thirds is wooded. Set on a low ridge between the valleys of the Lea and Roding, Epping Forest stretches for about 10 miles through London's outer suburban sprawl; a giant green oasis for the pleasure and recreation of city folk.

The history of Epping Forest can be traced back to the early twelfth century. Recorded as one of Henry I's forests, it was part of Waltham Forest, which in turn was one part of the Great Forest of Essex, for virtually the whole of the county was afforested by the Conqueror himself. The word 'forest' first appeared in the Domesday Book of 1086, where about twenty-five of them were mentioned, and derives from the Norman word *foris*, meaning 'outside' or 'without'. Contrary to popular belief, 'forest' does not necessarily signify a largely wooded tract of land (although often it was and still is). In actuality it was an area of jurisdiction outside or beyond the enclosures surrounding private dwellings or estates. In many cases this was open countryside, often poor land, unsuitable for agriculture, which was enclosed by the forest laws rather than physical barriers. The forests were established for the benefit of kings and nobility, preserving deer for the hunt as well as a ready source of timber, wood, grazing rights and even mineral rights. A hierarchy of forest officers administered the forest laws, drawing endless fines for a variety of misdemeanours, such as poaching, stealing timber or illegal grazing of livestock. These were all valuable commodities which raised funds for the Crown or provided gifts and sweeteners to obtain favours – far more useful than the odd day or two spent hunting. The complex history of forest politics throughout Britain, and the communities that lived in the forests, or in spite of them, is long and turbulent; and yet Epping and its people seem to have emerged relatively unscathed.

The nineteenth century was a time of dramatic developments and changes in Britain. An expanding population and an upsurge in agriculture and industry saw increasing demands upon land use, particularly in and around the cities. In 1851 the people of Epping must have been more than a trifle concerned as they saw the wholesale destruction of 90 per cent of nearby Hainault Forest, after it had been disafforested by Act of Parliament, in order to make way for agricultural land. Using huge steam ploughs, 1,000 years of landscape and habitat was erased in six weeks.

From 1860 the Crown allowed the manors around Epping to buy out the rights in their parishes, and over the next few years these private landowners proceeded to enclose many parts of the forest, thus excluding the commoners who had traditionally held the rights to lop and gather firewood and graze their livestock. A Commons Preservation Society was formed by a small group of far-sighted and public-spirited people to try and stem the tide, but the landowners were bullish, and by 1870 half of the 6,000 acres of the forest was enclosed. This was exacerbated when a bill was put before Parliament that would have permitted the eighteen lords of the manors to have the right to enclose 5,000 acres and, as a paltry compensation to the commoners, they offered 400 acres with rights, to be sold at market value, and 600 acres for public amenity. The Commons Preservation Society balked at this and was fortunate to get influential members of the Corporation of London to back its legal objections. Finances were also raised to fund what would turn out to be protracted legal proceedings, lasting three

A VIEW IN EPPING FOREST

A splendid engraving from 1871, showing many people out enjoying Epping Forest, with plenty of great old pollards all around. This was the year that proceedings were started by the Commoners in an attempt to stop the forest falling into private ownership. This image shows what a popular retreat it was for Londoners and fortunately by 1878 it had been saved for them in perpetuity by the Epping Forest Act.

years. On 24 November 1874 the case was found in favour of the commoners, and subsequently the Epping Forest Act of 1878 set aside the whole forest as a public open space in perpetuity, to be conserved by the Corporation of London. As Queen Victoria announced, during her visit on 6 May 1882 to open the forest formally to the public, 'It gives me the greatest satisfaction to dedicate this beautiful forest to the use and enjoyment of my people for all time.'

Up to this point Epping Forest had been evolving both naturally and through traditional management as heathland with wood pasture for the last 1,500 years. Suddenly, this all ceased. One of the Corporation's avowed aims was 'the maintenance of the Forest in its natural aspect', while another stipulation was 'the termination of the commoners' rights of lopwood'. Ignoring the fact that the forest probably hadn't looked 'natural' for centuries, a policy of non-intervention was followed until the late twentieth century with the best of motives, but to the detriment of biodiversity. High forest of oak, beech and hornbeam grew up, shading out much of the shrub layer and flora. Old pastures and heath were overtaken by scrub.

Recently, enlightened changes in woodland management have started to show very positive effects in the forest. Thinning and pollarding have opened up the canopy. In fact, the repollarding of some of the older trees has been a steep learning curve for today's foresters, as they have had to learn skills which had been neglected since before 1878. Pollarding old beeches and oaks needs the delicate touch – little and often, so as not to traumatize them. Many of the older trees will eventually die so a new generation of young pollards are being groomed to succeed. A grazing regime is ongoing, to maintain the pastures and encourage the flowers. There are now 650 different plant species alongside fifty different types of trees in Epping. More than 400 Red Data Book and nationally notable species of invertebrates are to be found and forty-eight breeding species of birds. The numerous ponds, many of which are flooded gravel pits, attract plentiful wildfowl, typically great crested grebes and goosanders. After all these years the fallow deer are still around too; a strain notable for their unusually dark colouring, perhaps they are direct descendants of those pursued by kings so long ago.

On reflection it seems as if this description of Epping Forest is heavily weighted towards its history, but in truth it is the very fortunate story of the salvation of a special environment for both people and wildlife, which could so easily have been lost for ever. To remember that ordinary people who are prepared to stand up and fight for a just cause really can win the day warms the cockles of the heart. The epic in Epping was in every sense a victory for the common man.

RIGHT The old beech pollards begin to burst forth with their vivid green spring foliage. Many of these groups, set closely together, are actually ancient coppice stools. These formations are known locally as coppards.

BELOW The rich autumnal colours in Epping Forest.

SILENT VALLEY NATURE RESERVE

A little–known woodland gem in the valleys of South Wales

There was no immediate sense of elevation; no hilltop vista with peerless countryside stretching to the horizon. If anything the approach was ever so slightly claustrophobic. Wedged between the narrow valley sides the village of Cwm, south of Ebbw Vale, typifies these communities lately bereft of their mining life-force, where row upon row of cheek-by-jowl, slab-fronted terraces stare bleakly into an uncertain future. Cendl Terrace, a small unremarkable street, swings abruptly uphill off the old main road, now sidestepped and bypassed by the new A4046. A short way up, a small car park on what appears to be an old mine tip sets you before the Silent Valley.

From this point on the countryside takes over. Most of the valley sides hereabouts are clad in conifers or oak woods, but the Silent Valley leads you to two very special woods – acclaimed as the most westerly and the highest-altitude beech woodlands in Britain.

The path enters the lower wood of Cwm Merddog right next to the babbling waters of the mountain stream, where craggy old beech pollards or long-neglected coppice stools hang precariously from the deeply cut banks. In the surrounding woodland beech predominates, but there is also oak, birch and, in the wetter flushes, alder. Most show signs of historic management. Tits and finches flit busily hither and yon, and surprisingly close at hand the yaffle of a green woodpecker startles, but, as usual, no sign of the perpetrator. Why are these beautiful birds so shy?

A variety of colour-coded paths lead through the woods. The blue path takes you onwards and upwards, passing a succession of glorious beeches, many of which will be 200 to 300 years old; some deliriously contorted specimens shaped by wood-cutting, the elements and time; others laid prone or bent double

by gales, trees grasping one another, or clenching the thin earth between silvery, claw-like roots.

You might be transported were it not for the growing rumble of distant machinery in this Silent Valley. Deeper into the woodland and the ground is increasingly decked in discarded plastic detritus – ragged carrier bags snag the boughs, brightly coloured sweetie and crisp wrappers peek from the drifts of beech leaves, yogurt pots, clingfilm, bubble wrap blow up the hillside and, if you're unlucky and the wind is from the north-west, the sickly smell of household rubbish and its attendant methane catches in the throat. Tragically, the land adjacent to the top of the Silent Valley is a massive landfill site. Obviously rubbish has to be disposed of somewhere and, in all fairness to the contractors who run the site, it is slowly being landscaped as it is filled in – some day in the future all will be covered over, the stench will subside and peace will return to the Silent Valley. In the meantime a 6-foot chain-link fence does keep people out of the landfill, but it simply is not good enough to keep the windblown rubbish out of the woods.

The uppermost wood of Coed Tyn-y-gelli has Site of Special Scientific Interest status, but the visual conflict between the beautiful old beech pollards and the confetti of plastic rubbish strewn right across the woodland floor is disheartening. Gwent Wildlife Trust is certainly doing a great job at this reserve, both with its woodland management and the encouragement of community and school-group participation. Its website (I am sure quite unintentionally) highlights this contast, for not only are visitors encouraged 'to study all the mini-beasts that work so hard reducing, re-using and recycling natural waste', but assistant project officer Morag

Late summer through the beeches in Cwm Merddog, in the Silent Valley.

OPPOSITE Amazing moss-clad roots of an ancient beech on the banks of Nant Merddog.

ABOVE Late summer turns to early autumn in this view from the nineteenth-century spoil heaps above the Silent Valley, looking down to the village of Cwm in the Ebbw Valley.

Boyd says: 'We hope children leave us with the understanding that everyone has some effect on the world around them. The key is to make sure your effect is positive; for example, by minimizing the amount of waste produced you can not only protect natural resources but also save money.'

Despite the environmental conflicts, the Silent Valley has much to offer. It really is a woodland site that is battling back from adversity. With the onset of the Industrial Revolution more than 200 years ago, a once-tranquil farming landscape was catapulted into a mining bonanza; remnants of the old tramline (or *dramline*, as it was known locally) still evident along the hillside, where coal from opencast or drift mines was transported down the valley. Some of the tumps are great waste tips (so no change there), long overgrown. Plentiful evidence of coppicing and pollarding, more so the latter, seems to indicate that sheep were frequently grazed here. Fuel wood was

taken and wood for charcoal to charge the forges of the ironworks. Today the summer slopes are clad with purple heather, special plants such as narrow buckler fern, heath spotted orchids and helleborines thrive, and a variety of mosses, liverworts and lichens find the atmosphere most favourable.

Winter may be a little stark here, and perhaps it isn't the best time for a first visit, but once the trees are in leaf and the flowers are bursting through you can forget the nearby tip and enjoy the ancient history of this wood, soaking up the marvellous westerly views across the valley and beyond.

CULTURAL CONNECTIONS

BISHAM WOODS

The inspiration for Kenneth Grahame's Wild Wood, high above the Thames near Marlow

Bisham Woods may well be familiar to many more people than have ever set foot there. For the thousands of motorists who regularly thrash along the A404, the quick cross-country cut between the M40 and M4, the woods dominate the eastward view. Although, strictly speaking, Bisham is just to the south of the Chilterns, it does have many characteristics typical of a Chiltern wood. Due to the particularly steep nature of the terrain, making it difficult for any form of agriculture, there has probably been woodland here for at least the last 500 years. Bisham actually comprises a number of small woods strung together, which are all basically beech woods with various localized variations; sometimes oak and ash, sometimes introduced conifers such as larch, Corsican pine or western red cedar.

For the most peaceful introduction to these beautiful woods it's best to find your way up on top of the hill, round the back, near Cookham Dean. Down pretty lanes with cottage gardens, the only stir may be the odd hedge trimmer or lawnmower in the distance or the cheeky yaffle of an invisible woodpecker – always so shy, both green and great spotted live here. The numerous well-used pull-ins for cars reflect the woods' popularity. The northernmost stretch, known as Quarry Wood, is perhaps the best served with a network of easy paths, and this wood, along with High Wood, Fultness Wood and Inkydown Wood to the south, comes within a Special Area of Conservation beech wood. This is reputedly the richest ancient woodland in Berkshire.

Whether it's sauntering beneath the eerie, emerald luminescence of the springtime beech canopy or kicking through the deep leaf fall, smelling autumn and revelling in its golden glow, this is a great place to be. A good mixture of high-forest trees along with old coppice stools and recent regeneration has created an interesting multi-generational wood, but much of this is not by design. The violent storms of 1987 and 1990 took a heavy toll on the beeches here. Many of these shallow-rooted trees fell before the blast, although in most places you'd be hard put to know how serious the devastation was. Like so many south-eastern beech woods, a fair bit of tidying up and replanting went on in the immediate aftermath, but nature (as ever) was the greatest healer, and natural regeneration far outstripped the planted trees. Ash and oak both find plenty of space here, along with hornbeam and hazel coppice, which adds to the biodiversity on the ground. There are some rare and special plants to be discovered, notably bird's-nest orchid, violet helleborine, green-flowered helleborine, yellow bird's-nest and thin-spiked wood sedge. And for all you snail enthusiasts out there, some of the snails (apparently) are pretty rare and ancient here too.

In the south-west corner of the woods sits a small ice house, built in the 1760s to provide Bisham Abbey with an early incarnation of the refrigerator. Here, ice gathered in winter was stored undergound to be used for chilling and preserving food as well as making things like ice cream. Recently restored, the building is open on the first Sunday of the month between May and September (however, visitors are advised to check with Bisham Parish Council, the keyholders, to save a wasted journey).

Bisham Woods have several claims to fame in the world of the creative arts. Author Kenneth Grahame, who grew up in nearby Cookham Dean in the late nineteenth century, spent much of his childhood exploring the Thames and the woods above. He drew on these formative experiences, and took Bisham as his inspiration for the Wild Wood in his classic children's book *The Wind in the Willows*. In 1817 the poet Percy Bysshe Shelley was living in Marlow

Sunlight glints through the high beech canopy in Bisham Woods.

OPPOSITE

TOP Tutsan, found in Bisham Woods, is a plant readily associated with ancient woodland. The strange name is thought to be derived from its French name 'toute-saine' – literally 'all wholesome', for the plant was known to the early herbalists for its healing virtues on grazes and wounds. An old name for the plant in Cornwall was 'touch-and-heal'.

BOTTOM Seldom found in any great number, although not nationally rare, nettle-leaved bellflower is an excellent indicator plant for ancient woodland, and may be found in these woods. Alternative names for the plant are bats-in-the-belfry or throatwort; the latter name redolent of its medicinal virtues for treating sore throats and tonsillitis.

BELOW An opening between the beeches reveals the view westward towards Marlow.

and regularly walked, read and wrote in these woods, and during the summer of that year he penned a controversial moral, political and theological poem here, which was published as *Laon and Cythna* (its original title was *The Revolt of Islam*). The celebrated artist Stanley Spencer, who was born in Cookham in 1891 and spent most of his life there, was known for his paintings of a religious nature – bizarrely, usually set in familiar locations and often peopled with local characters lightly disguised as figures from the Bible. Although Spencer is now renowned for these unusual paintings they were not particularly saleable in his lifetime so his agent persuaded him to paint landscapes. Around 1920 he made two paintings of Quarry Woods (sometimes titled Bisham Woods).

In 1889 Jerome K. Jerome's humorous account of a trip down the Thames – *Three Men in a Boat* – was published and is a perennially delightful, if dated, read:

Down to Cookham, past the Quarry Woods and the meadows, is a lovely reach. Dear old Quarry Woods! With your narrow, climbing paths, and little winding glades, how scented to this hour you seem with memories of sunny summer days! How daunted are your shadowy vistas with the ghosts of laughing faces! How from your whispering leaves there softly fall the voices of long ago!

Evocations, surely, of the mystery and magnificence of Grahame's Wild Wood.

Although the traffic noise below can sometimes be a little intrusive, there are some splendid views out of the woods across the River Thames, the nearby town of Marlow and the Chilterns Area of Outstanding Natural Beauty. If you're lucky, you may even spot a red kite soaring above.

SELBORNE HANGER

Beloved woods of the Reverend Gilbert White, celebrated Hampshire naturalist and diarist

The hanging woods of the Hampshire and Sussex borders, known as hangers, form a most distinctive landscape feature peculiar in its beech-dominated character to this part of the country. Steep valley sides are often densely wooded, largely because the terrain has always been too difficult for anything else other than woodland. Most of the peaceful little villages below the woods might have remained anonymous to this day had not the Reverend Gilbert White published his *Natural History and Antiquities of Selborne* in 1789. His wonderfully detailed observations of local natural history and village life are a classic text, which has never been out of print in more than 200 years.

Had it existed in the eighteenth century, the Hampshire Tourist Board could never have dreamt of a better emissary to promote the beauty and nature of this exquisite tract of countryside. There have been many changes in two centuries, but a certain essence of White's familiar Selborne lingers on. His description of the wood, as true today as then, is succinct yet intimate:

The high part of the south-west consists of a vast hill of chalk, rising 300 feet above the village, and is divided into a sheep-down, the High Wood, and a long hanging wood called The Hanger. The covert of this eminence is altogether Beech, the most lovely of all forest trees, whether we consider its smooth rind or bark, its glossy foliage or graceful pendulous boughs.

Early on a spring morning strike out for the top of the hanger, up the steep zigzag path that was there in White's day, and when you get there you're rewarded with cracking views out over the village and the surrounding countryside. A stroll along the crest of the hill takes you beneath the emerald shade of tall sinuous beeches, some of which could be 200 years old. Even though not these actual trees, the beeches of White's hanger must have been of similar character, and the abundance of tiny beech seedlings all over the woodland floor alerts you to the irrepressible struggle for reproduction. How many seeds must a tree drop? How many germinate? How many are eaten? How many survive? Only when a gap opens in the canopy and light floods in does a single beech sapling have the ghost of a chance of making it to a mature tree. Tread softly and watch for the roe deer which thrive up here – you may well catch them breakfasting on a young beech.

The calcareous soils of the chalk support some particularly rare and beautiful flowers, including green hellebore, bird's-nest orchid, violet helleborine, green-flowered helleborine and stinking hellebore. The latter plant has long been popular with gardeners; in fact Gilbert White admitted transplanting a few to his own garden. Its real boon is that it has evergreen leaves and blooms in January, when few flowers are flourishing. The 'stinking' epithet refers to a slightly foetid aroma. The plant was a valuable asset to the old herbalists. Culpeper knew it as the black hellebore (also Christmas herb or Christmas flower) and cites the roots as 'very effectual against all melancholy diseases, especially such as are of long standing, as quartan agues, and madness; it helps the falling sickness, the leprosy, both the yellow and black jaundice, the gout, sciatica, and convulsions …' In White's time he reports that 'the good women give the leaves powdered to children troubled with worms; but it is a violent remedy, and ought to be administered with caution.'

Beyond the lip of the hill lies Selborne Common, which is White's 'sheep-down', an area of acidic soils, rather than the chalk on the hanger itself. This was once grazed as wood pasture, as the numerous

Early sunlight glances through the beeches shading the path which runs across the top of Selborne Hanger. You almost expect to meet the Reverend Gilbert White strolling towards you, lost in contemplation on such a glorious morning in his natural demesne.

old beech pollards attest, but the practice was abandoned around 1950. Most of these pollards are long outgrown, yet they still reflect the historic management of the common and provide valuable wildlife habitats. Some have collapsed or died, so in order to maintain the landscape character the National Trust has begun to form new pollards out of maiden trees (those that have previously been left to their own devices). Although there are a few open spaces, much of the tree cover is quite dense, with an abundance of oak, ash, field maple, ancient hawthorns and frequently a thick understorey of holly. Again, the National Trust is trying to reinvigorate the grassland on the common by reintroducing grazing cattle. If the flowers receive a helping hand more butterflies will return. Already there are rare species such as Duke of Burgundy, silver-washed fritillary, green and purple hairstreak and, very occasionally, purple emperor and white admiral to be discovered.

Ancient woodland indicator species, such as yellow archangel and wood anemone, are still to be found in profusion, which reveals that woodland has held sway here for centuries, but archaeologists have also detected ancient field patterns on the common, which they think may go back to Romano-Britain or

even earlier. Earth banks around the perimeter are thought to be medieval, while another earth bank running across the common has been dated to the mid-eighteenth century and is assumed to have been part of a protective enclosure around a coppiced compartment. An old dew pond near the western boundary must once have been used by those who grazed livestock up here.

As you ramble around the many paths on Selborne Common there is a strong sense of walking through history. Blink for a second and you're back to Gilbert White's bucolic idyll. Surely we should let the great man have the last word, from his poem 'The Invitation to Selborne':

Me far above the rest Selbornian scenes,
The pendent forests, and the mountain greens,
Strike with delight: there spreads the distant view,
That gradual fades till sunk in misty blue:
Here nature hangs her slopy woods to sight,
Rills purl between, and dart a quivering light.

ELEPHANTINE BEECHES

BURNHAM BEECHES

Ancient pollards in Buckinghamshire; surely the most famous beech trees in Britain

This great old pollard in Burnham Beeches may be hollow, but in the top right corner of the cavity it's possible to discern an aerial root growing down towards the ground.

It's easy to take somewhere like Burnham Beeches for granted in this day and age, but history reveals that its fate could tragically have taken completely different turns in the past, and the whole magical landscape could easily have been lost.

Perhaps the earliest mention by name of the Burnham Beeches is found in Jacob George Strutt's *Sylva Britannica* of 1830. Strutt's delightful wood engraving clearly depicts the stunted, hollowed and contorted frames of the eponymous pollards. Strutt makes note of Thomas Gray (he of 'Elegy Written in a Country Churchyard' fame) and his correspondence with Horace Walpole in 1737, where he waxes lyrically upon his visit:

I have at the distance of half a mile, through a green lane, a forest (the vulgar call it a common) all my own, at least as good as so, for I spy no human thing in it but myself ... both vale and hill are covered with most venerable beeches, and other very reverend vegetables, that, like most other ancient people, are always dreaming out their old stories to the winds.

Indeed, Burnham Beeches appears on eighteenth- and nineteenth-century maps as a common, and would have been largely composed of heathland and grass for grazing livestock; the trees managed as pollards in a wood-pasture regime. Oak as well as beech were regularly pollarded from about 1500 to 1820, when the need for fuel wood was eclipsed by coal. Beech are by far the more abundant of the two species here. It is estimated that there may have been as many as 3,000 beech pollards growing at Burnham in the seventeenth century and, even today, around 450 still survive – trees which are generally adjudged to be around 400 years old, an exceptional age for beech.

In exactly the same way as Gray was enchanted by the ancient beeches 250 years ago, anyone visiting today can't fail to be equally swept away by the rugged beauty of these trees and truly amazed by their tenacity. Most are hollow, many partially rotted away, some broken, bowed or prostrate, but the life-force still bursts from within them each and every spring. Some of the hollowed boles reveal aerial roots creeping earthward, seeking fresh purchase and renewed vigour in the rich loam long-gathered inside the tree base. Other pollards are high-level homes to arboreal intruders and chancers – holly, rowan and elder; avian introductions of a beakful that went astray.

It seems inconceivable now, but the 540 acres of Burnham Beeches might have been swallowed up by private landowners in the mid-nineteenth century (and who knows what 'improvements') had not the Kyrle Society stepped in to prevent development and, subsequently, the Corporation of London seized the opportunity to purchase the site in 1879, with a clear purpose of conserving it for the perpetual enjoyment of the public; a management role it still pursues most effectively to this day.

It also seems strange to think that some people saw no merit in the glorious forms of the old pollards. Before the First World War some committee of old buffers wanted to tidy the place up and get rid of all the rotten, dangerous old trees. Fate intervened (and probably the war) and before final decisions were made and anything terrible could happen to the trees the committee had all died. During the mid-twentieth century there were writers who were evidently not at all tuned in to ancient trees. John Rodgers in his *English Woodland* viewed the pollards as mutilated – 'for a mutilation it is, however much the pollarding may conserve their life. In comparison with the bulky trunk the branches seem thin and

77

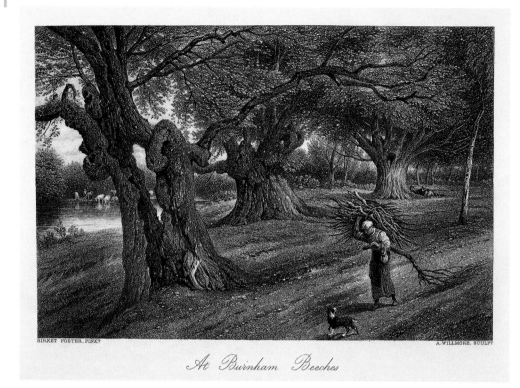

BIRKET FOSTER, PINX?   A.WILLMORE, SCULP?

At Burnham Beeches

scraggy.' Even the forester and prolific author H.L. Edlin seemed less than impressed by these trees, also considering their forms as a mutilation, and passing quickly on to his beloved timber trees he concedes: 'Since we shall never produce their like again, we may well preserve small areas as curiosities.'

In recent years we have come to understand so much more about these types of ancient trees and their significance in the cultural history, landscape and ecology of the countryside. With due concern about the future of Burnham's appearance and its various habitats, the rangers have embarked upon a whole new regime of pollarding to keep the old trees going as long as possible and to introduce new pollards to carry the mantle in the future. Bearing in mind that pollarding beech trees ceased more than a hundred years ago in Britain, there was a very steep learning curve for everyone involved. Early attempts at cutting back all the boughs of the old timers generally traumatized the trees completely and they usually died. Now the practice is to cut a few branches back every few years, keeping the trees in balance and leaving some foliage to sustain them between loppings. There have also been reintroductions of pigs, cattle and sheep in selective compartments in an effort to re-create the original wood-pasture regime … and there are useful information boards to explain exactly what's going on.

There are many elements to enjoy at Burnham Beeches – lots of open space, ideal for letting off steam, soaking up some sun or spreading out a picnic; as well as coppice woods, winding paths, high forest, secret valleys, sink holes, bogs and long-forgotten boundary banks to discover. The level nature of the terrain also makes Burnham a great place for those who are less able and agile to get into the woods.

Whatever you choose to do you will still go home with a string of vivid images stored away of the weird old beeches. Not only was Thomas Gray moved by them, but also the composer Felix Mendelssohn – the tree beneath which he is believed to have sat to compose *Midsummer Night's Dream* succumbed in 1990 (his presence lives on in Mendelssohn Slope), and the Swedish Nightingale, Jenny Lind, also adopted her own tree where she would practise her arias, this one long gone. Named trees such as His Majesty – a monster with a 30-foot girth which crashed to earth in the great storm of 1987 – and the Elephant Tree, alas, are no more, but the Cage Pollard courted international fame in the American feature film production *Robin Hood: Prince of Thieves* as recently as 1991.

Finding such a wealth of ancient beech pollards on the very edge of the Chilterns, arguably Britain's beech stronghold, begs the question as to whether much of the high forest, encouraged to service the furniture trade of the nineteenth century, may previously have contained similar communities of such trees. Ashridge, in Hertfordshire, offers a glimpse.

ABOVE
LEFT A superb engraving by A. Willmore, from a Miles Birket Foster original, of the ancient pollards at Burnham Beeches, c1880. The Victorians were equally as fascinated as we are today by these remarkable old stagers.

RIGHT Male and female flowers of beech emerge, perform their pollinating business, and seem to be gone in a trice.

OPPOSITE Autumn colour in one of the clearings. It's not all beech though. To the right a fine whitebeam is laden with scarlet fruits. The fence in the distance is part of a recent grazing regime, using sheep and cattle in limited compartments, with the intention of resurrecting the heathland and encouraging the flora.

SAVERNAKE FOREST

A record-breaking avenue through the beechen groves of Wiltshire

Beech has become so widespread across Britain, featuring in every aspect of the landscape, both for function and ornament, that it has often been assumed to have native status throughout the country. This is not altogether the case, for ancient pollen records, which are less than plentiful for beech, seem to indicate that earliest colonization dates from about 6000BC, but only across the southern counties of England, with odd outliers in south-east Wales. Suffice to say that beech made it to Britain just before the land bridge to Europe disappeared, so it is a legitimate native, if only in southern England. The subsequent story of the advance of beech has been accelerated by human influence combined with a natural propensity to regenerate readily from seed. The tree's success on a variety of different soils, as far north as Aberdeenshire, would seem to indicate that the species would have colonized naturally anyway given time.

There are many naturally occurring beech woods in the southern counties of England, but with a few exceptions most currently have the feel of relatively recent plantations, rather than ancient woodlands, where coppice wood was once cut for fuel and high-forest trees provided timber for the furniture industry over the last 200 years, particularly in the nineteenth century. Places like Burnham Beeches (see page 77), liberally scattered with ancient pollards, are rare finds indeed. Oak and beech often coexist, but oak takes longer to reach maturity than beech, and has to get a head start on the young beeches as it cannot thrive in the deep shade beneath them.

Hard by the delightful market town of Marlborough in Wiltshire lies the Savernake Forest, where the overriding impression today is of a vast beech wood, attended by oaks and stands of conifers, but this was not always its composition. Earliest mention of the name dates back to 934 where 'crofts alongside the woodland called Safernoc' were parcels of land awarded to the Abbey of Wilton by King Athelstan. Savernake is thought to be derived from 'Severn oak' (Severn being a common river name). Straight away this suggests that oak was the predominant tree 1,000 years ago. First established as a royal forest in 1067, Savernake's boundaries and fortunes have fluctuated with events in history and the variable attentions of a long, continuous lineage of some thirty-one generations of hereditary wardens stretching back to Richard Esturmy, to whom William the Conqueror first granted the forest.

Until the beginning of the eighteenth century it would appear that Savernake was a mixture of heath, wood pasture with a few old oak pollards and scattered areas of neglected coppice. Generally, the trees and woodlands were poorly managed and unkempt. From 1703 a period of tree planting and landscape enhancement altered the face of the forest. The renowned Lancelot 'Capability' Brown was called in by the 3rd Earl of Ailesbury to make some changes on a grand scale. Perhaps grandest of all was a remarkable avenue of towering beech trees – the Grand Avenue – which runs for almost 4 miles from the King's Way (now better known as the A4) to the Ailesburys' ancestral home at Tottenham House. It is still recognized as the longest avenue in Britain today, but has suffered a little over the years. Some trees have died, others have been wind thrown – about 700 beeches throughout the forest were lost in the 1990 gales, but regular replanting endeavours to maintain the character of this unique feature.

There are many other eighteenth-century rides and avenues that were cut through the forest, eight of which meet up midway along the Grand Avenue

Low sunlight strikes across this winter view of the beeches along the Grand Avenue through the middle of Savernake Forest.

at Eight Walks, where each of the 'spokes of the wheel' conform exactly to the points of the compass. All around you the silvery-grey, elephantine trunks of the beeches stretch eagerly aloft, greedy for the light. This meeting place, this focal point in the forest, feels as if something more is required – some landmark or a monument perhaps. The Earl once had plans for an impressive lodge or pavilion here, with windows looking down each avenue, but it came to nought. Of more sinister account is the record of a gibbet being sited here in the sixteenth century, surmounted by a pair of ram's horns, a dark memorial to the execution of a notorious sheep thief called Brathwaite.

A great deal of the surrounding woodland is composed of beech, but its origins are of anything but a natural or ancient beech wood. Some of the oldest beeches are long-outgrown pollards, which must reflect the wood-pasture regime that was beginning to be eclipsed beneath much of the ornamental planting of the early eighteenth century. Many of the trees might well have been pollarded up to the latter part of the nineteenth century, yet some of the most awesome examples are those with great fists of upthrust stems, probably ignored by foresters for over 150 years, their sprawling, fluted boles braced in the soft, springy wood floor. At the other end of the scale there are numerous plantations of relatively young beech trees, planted by the Forestry Commission, since it took a lease on Savernake in 1939.

In some parts of the forest there are traces of the original denizens – massive, crumbling ancient oak pollards; a few of the largest may even date back to the eleventh century. Although the naturalists and tree lovers of the nineteenth century celebrated such forest giants as the King Oak, the Queen Oak, the Creeping Oak and the Duke's Vaunt Oak, these are all now long gone, but fortunately recorded for posterity in several fine old engravings. Today, the most famous tree in Savernake must be the Big Belly Oak (also known as the Decanter Oak), which countless motorists will recognize as the monster that sits so perilously close to the main Marlborough to Salisbury road. With a girth of 36 feet, best guesstimates of its age are around 1,100 years.

Diligent exploration of Savernake's beautiful woodland will reveal numerous other ancient oaks hidden away in the depths. Some still thrive, while others are dying or dead. Mid-twentieth-century

Sadly this great old oak pollard has eventually died. It might be that it had actually run its natural span, but the close proximity of the beeches probably didn't help matters. Even in death this will still continue to be a treasure house of invertebrate life and, very likely, a splendid bat roost.

A massive outgrown beech pollard, uncut for well over a century, caught by the late afternoon sunlight,

A carpet of bluebells stretches into the distance beneath this stand of beech.

planting seems to have paid little respect to the oaks and many were far too densely surrounded with plantations of beech or conifers. More enlightened times have seen many of them given room to flourish, and a few have responded, but even the dead oaks are still hugely important as habitat for invertebrates, birds and bats.

No matter what time of year you visit Savernake, there's always something to entrance, and with 4,500 acres to explore you're hardly likely to run out of space. In spring there are phenomenal displays of bluebells and in autumn the forest is renowned for its fungi, which have led to 905 acres being designated as a Site of Special Scientific Interest. Both roe and fallow deer roam the woods and rare birds such as nightjars, woodcock and nightingales all frequent the forest, with occasional sightings of red kites, honey buzzards and goshawks. During the summer months, one small compartment is currently being grazed by seven White Park cattle as part of an experiment to study the impact of grazing on the flora and fauna of the woodland floor. So don't be alarmed or confused if you happen upon these beautiful white beasts with their sooty black noses peering back at you through the trees – they really are meant to be there.

FLORAL GEMS

DYMOCK WOODS

Unrivalled displays of wild daffodils in Gloucestershire

A few miles south of the village of Dymock in Gloucestershire lies Dymock Wood and a knot of associated woodlands that straddle the ceaseless roar of the M50. Thankfully, the motorway runs through a cutting most of the way, so unless you are very close the noise is seldom too imposing. Hurtling back and forth between the Midlands and South Wales you might notice that several miles of the verges here are speckled with daffodils in mid March, and would probably assume that the Highways Department had planted the bulbs. What you see are the edges of ancient woodland, amazingly, still well endowed with one of Britain's rarest wild flowers. It is well worth taking a diversion to seek out a little more of this botanical curiosity.

Barely a stone's throw from the motorway incredible carpets of wild daffodils deck the woodland floor in early spring. These tiny feral blooms, petite and delicate in comparison to their larger, flamboyant, cultivated cousins, may not be nationally unique to these woods, but undoubtedly this is the very best location in Britain in which to see them en masse. The country lanes south of Dymock and neighbouring Kempley prime your expectation with numerous clumps and drifts of daffodils along hedges and ditches, while you occasionally come upon an old orchard or meadow where the undisturbed greensward is full to bursting with flowers. This might be a brief insight into what the landscape might have looked like hereabouts, before farmland was ploughed and improved and before many hedges and woods were grubbed out.

Dymock Wood, Oxenhall Wood, Hay Wood and Queen's Wood all contain wonderful displays, but often the greatest concentrations of flowers are around the woodland perimeters and along the paths and rides, where sunlight gets to the ground; as for some years these woods have been commercially managed for softwood production, with large compartments of conifers, beneath which the ground flora is relatively sparse and the species limited.

For the most intense daffodil experience you need to explore some of the smaller woods; most particularly those which have retained more of their complement of broadleaved trees. Betty Dawes Wood at Four Oaks is an absolute cracker with a lovely circular path providing the perfect tour. Sadly, nobody seems to know who Betty might have been, although the assumption must be that she was once the owner of the wood. A little to the south, the woods of Shaw Common might just contain the ultimate cloth of gold. Great drifts of daffodils adorn the broad track leading you on until you breast a gentle rise and all before you is shining yellow, almost as far as you can see through the wood. Some handsome oak standards, hazel coppice and the occasional dark sentinel holly complete the picture. It seems hard to believe that barely a month earlier the woodland floor lay brown and seemingly lifeless, before each of the tiny powerhouse bulbs spiked the oak-leaf litter with their blue-green daggers and tightly sealed buds; each one eager to burst its bold golden trumpet; a celebration of life renewed for yet another year. Caught by the breeze they dance – a corps de ballet commanding this natural arena.

The earliest botanical authorities were largely the herbals, and notably John Gerard in his *Herball or Generall Historie of Plantes* of 1597 states that 'the yellow English Daffodil grows almost every where through England'. Geoffrey Grigson in *The Englishman's Flora* of 1958 questions the reliability

A superb carpet of wild daffodils beneath some majestic oak standards on Shaw Common.

of Gerard's assertion, for he was not apparently known for his extensive travels through the realm. However, a variety of accounts from the nineteenth century seem to indicate that wild daffodils were reasonably common throughout the country. So why should the plant's decline or, more especially, its retrenchment to just a few localized colonies have been so marked over the last century? Grigson was puzzled, but suggested drainage schemes, grassland improvement, grubbing out of ancient woods (certainly still a big problem when he was writing) and even transplanting – there have always been people keen to acquire new plants for their gardens with little thought of the consequences to wild populations. Thankfully, legislation has put a stop to most of this today.

Nevertheless the present rarity of wild daffodils nationally seems hard to explain for they are clearly tenacious little plants, and have often survived in places where there is no longer any woodland cover. Barely 6 miles north of Dymock the sweeping open pastures around Woolhope Cockshoot boast impressive swathes of wild daffodils, among which the leaves of wood anemone wait to succeed. Both plants are noted as indicator species for ancient woodland. While it is possible that they have always grown in these unimproved pastures (an 1845 map certainly shows this as open ground at that time) this area may equally have been part of the nearby Haugh Wood system (see page 32), and been cleared of trees hundreds of years ago. Conversely, exploration of much of the interior of the present Haugh Wood, almost all of which does have ancient origins, shows very little evidence of wild daffodils. The management regime of the mid-twentieth century, much of it with dense stands of conifers, was hardly ideal for ancient woodland flowers, but it's hard to know exactly how widespread the daffodils might once have been.

Until 1959, when the local railway line closed, masses of visitors from London and the West Midlands came by train every year to see the spectacle around Dymock; the line being affectionately known as the Daffodil Line. Not only did these tourists return home with arms and baskets full of daffs, but there was also a nice little business shipping boxes of them up to the capital for sale in the flower markets. Today it's Daffodil Teas at the village halls and even an official Daffodil Way circular walk which takes in some of the very

best places to view the flowers, but there are lots of paths all over the local woods and fields, so you can simply please yourself, wandering and wondering at one of the finest natural floral displays anywhere in Britain.

BELOW What would appear to have once been an old orchard, Gwen and Vera's Fields, on the edge of Shaw Common, contain a superb display of wild daffodils.

OPPOSITE Wild daffodils after an early morning shower in Dymock Wood.

A brief burst of sunshine in Hayley Wood illuminates this little clump of oxlips.

HAYLEY WOOD

Rare and delicate, the flowers of oxlip abound in a Cambridgeshire wood

Along the gentle undulations of the B1046 between Longstowe and Little Gransden, in Cambridgeshire, keep your eyes open for a water tower. There are several beautiful and ancient woods in this part of the county, but viewed from a distant road their low profiles in the landscape all look rather similar, and seldom signal which are the very best ones to visit. The water tower, and it is unmissable, tells you that you've arrived. On the opposite side of the road a track leads down to Hayley Wood, flanked on the east by a medieval hedgerow, but it's only a short walk to floral heaven and a historic ancient woodland.

As you cross the long-defunct trackbed of the old Cambridge to Bedford railway line a deer-proof gateway admits you to what is known as the Triangle. This, unlike the majority of Hayley, is predominantly an oak wood with hawthorn, birch and sallow and quite a poor ground flora – certainly little sign of the ancient woodland indicators that grow in the older part. Apparently this area was originally laid to arable and only in the 1920s did it become wooded. Take a moment to be quite impressed at how eighty years has transformed this piece of land, but keep walking . . .

You soon arrive at another deer fence and enter Hayley Wood proper, crossing the original bank and ditch. This ancient woodland has a long continuous history of management, which Oliver Rackham has traced back to the mid-thirteenth century, and he even suggests that there is a reference to the wood in the Domesday Book. Extracts from the *Ely Coucher Book* of 1251 clearly refer to coppicing in Hayley Wood (or *Boscus de Heyle*, as it was then called), the use of its underwood for fuel and hurdle-making and the protective earth bank around the wood's perimeter. After a chequered history the wood was eventually acquired by the local Wildlife Trust in 1962 so its future is now assured.

Spring is undoubtedly one of the best times to visit. Regular coppice management of the compartments, which make up the wood, perfectly illustrates how floral regeneration responds to the coppicing cycles and the levels of light and shade that result. Find a point along one of the broad rides where you can compare tree and ground cover in several different compartments. Where the tree cover is fairly dense, even after as little as ten years, the flowers are relatively sparse. Where trees have grown up for four or five years the flowers are there, but concentrated more so in the sunnier gaps between the trees. In those areas recently cut over, the second year after coppicing produces the most glorious carpet of wild flowers. The plants use that first summer after coppicing to gather their energy before bursting forth in full floral glory the following season.

Although there are many of the usual flower species associated with ancient woodland here – wood anemone, dog's mercury, bluebell, dog-violet and early-purple orchid – the floral star of this wood is the oxlip. Although the plant was originally noted in the mid-seventeenth century, growing in Cambridgeshire, it was originally thought to be a hybrid between primrose and cowslip (there is such a plant – the false oxlip – *Primula veris* x *vulgaris*) rather than a separate species. However, further investigation by two Essex botanists, George Gibson and Henry Doubleday, in the 1840s, concluded that the oxlip (*Primula elatior*) truly was a distinct species, as they discovered it growing in profusion where no primroses existed. Since that time it has been recorded in a fairly confined area on the boulder-clay of East Anglia – principally parts of north Essex, west Suffolk and Cambridgeshire, and almost exclusively within ancient woodland. Gibson and Doubleday found meadows full of the plant in the nineteenth century, but the relentless march of

ABOVE Ancient ash coppice stool on an old boundary bank near the edge of the wood.

RIGHT Early purple orchids are plentiful and, like the oxlips, a good indicator of ancient woodland.

OPPOSITE
TOP One of the strange low cut ash pollards is already bewhiskered by healthy new growth. Close examination shows that some of the lower shoots have already been nibbled by deer or rabbits, but the top ones should get away unscathed. In the background is a fine crab apple – a fairly rare tree here, but a good indicator of ancient woodland.

BOTTOM Lesser celandine share the woodland floor with oxlips, part of the stupendous display for which Hayley Wood is so rightly famed. This compartment is inside one of the deer fences . . . the only way these pretty little flowers can avoid being eaten. Other woods near Hayley, which have no deer fences, have no oxlips.

agriculture meant that such sights disappeared long ago. Because of its close association with ancient woods, when it does appear in hedgerows or field margins today, it's a pretty good bet that the land was once woodland – a fact that studies of old maps usually bear out.

A combination of the ongoing coppicing and the exclusion of deer at Hayley Wood have been the main reasons for the spectacular displays of this rare and beautiful little flower each April. Visits to other ancient woods in the area, where deer are rampant and the coppicing regime has not been maintained, often shows evidence of the plants, but seldom with any flowers. A dramatic example of this came to light during a visit to nearby Knapwell Wood; a striking photograph of which featured in Peter Marren's *Woodland Heritage* – a yellow carpet of oxlips stretching into the distance among the newly coppiced trees, but that was in 1971. In 2008 barely a single flower could be found – there was dense tree cover and easy access for the deer, populations of which have swelled in the last forty years.

Hayley is basically an ash, field maple and hazel wood with accompanying oak standards, and a walk around will uncover much of its ancient history. Although there are not many earthworks within the wood, most of the original boundary bank and its external ditch still survives – perhaps most impressive around the south-west corner. Here you will also find some of the largest ash coppice stools, undoubtedly several hundred years old. In the north-west quarter of the wood there is an armed pond, a deliberate, but extremely old construction, and assumed to have been used for watering cattle. At one or two points around the wood's boundary there are smaller, irregularly shaped ponds, presumably for the same purpose. Watch out too for the pink, sweet-scented blossom of the occasional old crab apple – small trees (they grow extremely slowly), but they are very old.

Four broad, straight tracks run through the wood that meet at the 'roundabout', which is apparently where the logging horses were turned when extracting timber. There is also a useful information board here and a little shelter if the heavens open. The clay holds the water in Hayley Wood, which is ideal for the trees and plants, but it can make for quite squishy walking – sturdy boots definitely required.

FORESTS FOUND AND FAMED

WENTWOOD FOREST

A vast forgotten forest of Gwent emerges from obscurity

Sherwood Forest may be the most famous forest, largely because of its legendary associations with Robin Hood, and it is visited by multitudes every year. The New Forest (now a National Park) is England's largest forest by area, and Epping Forest is the playground for Londoners. The Dean, Savernake, the Wyre and those treasured pine-clad fragments of the Caledonian Forest are all familiar friends, but where does Wentwood fit into our gazetteer of British forests? Most people would be hard pressed to say they had ever heard of it, let alone where it is.

That is until 2006, when some 900 acres of Wentwood came on to the market. This represented a little over a third of the existing 3,000 acres of forest which straddles the hills between the Usk Valley and the Wye Valley, reaching to within 5 miles of Newport at its southern extremity. Here then was the ancient forest that once divided the old kingdom of Gwent into Gwent Uwchcoed and Gwent Iscoed (above and below the wood). By 2005 the majority of the forest was effectively one gigantic conifer plantation, but the Woodland Trust saw beneath this and believed that, given time and the right kind of sympathetic management, it could be returned to its glorious broadleaf status. An appeal for £1.5 million was launched and in 2006 the Trust completed the deal, with the generous help of several other partners.

The history of Wentwood is not easily unravelled, as early references are at best sketchy. William Linnard, an authority on Welsh woodland and trees, tells us that the woods of Wentwood (Coit Guent) were mentioned in *The Book of Llandaff* during the Dark Ages, but they do not achieve forest status – that is, an area of jurisdiction – until the area came under the control of the Marcher Lords shortly after the Norman Conquest. Wentwood was then presided over by a strict and sometimes punitive hierarchy of Foresters' Courts with their duly appointed officers to attend to all matters of venison and vert – basically the management and supervision of the game and the trees. Forest laws were not to be trifled with and the common folk met with harsh penalties for infringements such as poaching, theft or unauthorized tree felling. Records tell us that some poor unfortunate condemned as late as 1829 was hanged from one of the Foresters' Oaks.

Until the latter part of the seventeenth century all must have been relatively harmonious in Wentwood – the local nobility could hunt in their forest as well as earn revenue from timber for construction purposes, coppice wood for charcoal and bark for the tanneries; while the commoners had rights, established since the reign of Henry III, to take hay-bote (wood for hedging), wood-bote (fuel wood), pannage (grazing pigs on acorns or beech mast) and herbage (grazing livestock on grass). Then, in 1678, Henry, Earl of Worcester and Raglan, decided to enclose 7,000 acres of Wentwood for red deer. He also was reputed to have felled £60,000 worth of timber and even managed to prosecute sixty-four tenants for various offences. Perhaps this set the pattern for the next 300 years.

One of the earliest accounts of Wentwood comes from William Coxe in his *Historical Tour of Monmouthshire* (1801). He recalls:

'The Forest Chase of Wentwood formerly was considerable for its extent, jurisdiction, members and dependencies, as it was supreme over all the chases and woodlands adjacent and for its lofty and proud oaks and stately and large beeches, which the soil doth naturally and luxuriously produce, intermixed with the venerable Holly (which was criminal for any to cut down), the

The Curley Oak – probably the oldest tree in Wentwood Forest, this old stager is hanging on amid the conifers. In recent times foresters have felled a few of the closest trees (see stump behind) to let a bit more light get to the old tree and increase its chances of survival.

several eminencies, brows and ranges throughout the extent thereof, make a commanding and agreeable landskip …'

However, Coxe tempers this lyrical historic overview with his own findings, remarking upon 'the deep gloom of this dreary and uninhabited district'. The distinguished ruralist author H.J. Massingham, visiting in 1952, came to much the same conclusion. He begins: 'If the gloom was deep a century and a half ago, it is Stygian today.' The last big trees of Wentwood had been felled during the Second World War so, as Massingham bemoans,

'All has been now so savagely cut over that hardly a tree is to be seen except the conifers of the Forestry Commission, themselves to be clear-felled … Everywhere I saw the voids where trees once stood, filled in with a litter of bramble, willowherb and tussocky whitegrass. The haughty woodland nymph intoxicating in her wild ways has become a raddled cast-off slut. The whole area is a dismal derelict waste, an upland hell and the bleakest of monuments to man's suicidal folly and cupidity.'

In the open areas of Wentwood, previously cleared of conifers, the natural regeneration of birch and broom is impressive and beautiful.

An ancient beech pollard on an old boundary bank on the northern edge of the forest. The beeches here may well be over 200 years old and, judging by the size of the boughs, have probably not been pollarded since the 19th century.

Surrounded by the heady scent of bluebells, old beech pollards mark the north-east boundary of the forest.

The picture is vivid. Could it get any worse?

Thankfully not, for the stewardship of the Forestry Commission over the intervening years has seen a period of relative stability return to Wentwood. Granted, the vast majority of the woodland is conifers, but there has been no further erosion of those last little vestiges of the original broadleaf cover and ancient woodland flora which continue to hang on at the margins. If anything, the last period of dramatic change had been during the late nineteenth and early twentieth centuries. Before this most of the forest had been turned over to coppice, to convert to charcoal for the iron industry, but this need had been eclipsed by the use of coke in the later nineteenth century, and thus broadleaf coppice woods began to be converted into coniferous plantations from about 1880. Right up to the 1960s it was conifers which continued to be planted at the expense of broadleaved trees.

So to walk through Wentwood today is something of a treasure hunt to seek out what is left of the original woodland as it might have looked before 1880. One must bear in mind that many of the commentators of the nineteenth century were affronted by the prospect of coppiced or pollarded trees, which most of us find entrancing today. In the depths of the wood watch out for the mighty old Curley Oak. (Nobody knows for sure how it got its name, but it is said that the nineteenth-century map surveyors often asked local inhabitants what the familiar name for some local feature might be and, as such, it then appeared on the maps.) Along the northern margins long-outgrown beech pollards form gargantuan forgotten hedges on top of old wood banks, while others grasp the steep slopes above the Usk Valley. In March wild daffodils burst through the leaf litter, and a little later swathes of bluebells will wash across many clearings.

Just a few hundred yards from the Curley Oak you'll find a charming little dell, where a stream trickles playfully beneath oaks and beeches and wild flowers are quickly reclaiming the newly opened ground – a marked contrast to the wasteland below the conifers. This typifies the bright, exciting future here for ancient woodland that has been subjugated for so long beneath a vast timber farm. From an obscure, forgotten forest, Wentwood is poised to become one of the greatest places on the Welsh borders to get away from it all and unwind in the woods.

SHERWOOD FOREST

Ancient oaks of Nottinghamshire impart the spirit of Robin Hood

Most people think of Sherwood as a forest of oaks, but in reality the largest ancient part of the forest called Birkland is really a birch wood, which grew originally from heathland. Here an ancient dead oak stands amid the birch like some totem of a long-lost tribe.

The New Forest may be Britain's largest and arguably most famous forest, but it is Sherwood Forest which conjures the greatest affection in the hearts of the British people. If for no other reason, it's for those rose-tinted tales of Robin Hood and his band of honest-to-goodness, not-so-nasty outlaws, who righted wrongs and stole from the rich to give to the poor, that Sherwood has remained uppermost in so many people's childhood memories. Who could forget the hunky, wholesome Richard Greene winning through each week in the long-running 1950s TV series *The Adventures of Robin Hood*? In 1991 the role fell to Kevin Costner in *Robin Hood: Prince of Thieves* and, apparently, Hollywood is about to launch RH once more.

Separating the myth from reality of Robin Hood has taxed scholars for centuries. A general consensus has usually set him in the thirteenth century, although various accounts, largely drawn from ballads and folklore, also place him as late as the sixteenth century. In the nineteenth century the historian and antiquarian the Reverend Joseph Hunter asserted that Robin Hood was no myth, but a supporter of the Earl of Lancaster in the early fourteenth century. When the Earl was executed for treason in 1322, Hunter believed that Robin Hood and his followers retreated into their shady existence in Sherwood Forest, where they survived through poaching and extorting money from passing travellers for safe passage. However, contemporary records from the thirteenth and fourteenth centuries fail to make any mention of his existence so, generally speaking, he must simply remain an archetype; a medieval renegade, living in the shadows with his cohorts.

The Sherwood Forest of today actually bills itself as a country park, and one with a very strong Robin Hood theme at its core. The visitor centre is keen to attract families, so it has skilfully embraced both the romance of Robin and the natural history of the forest to encourage children to explore and learn (without them really realizing it, because they're having fun). There are lots of special events on offer, particularly in the summer months, encompassing both history and nature.

There is an excellent network of well-surfaced paths, all on extremely level terrain, so no matter what your age or ability you can easily explore the whole forest. However, it's also pretty exciting to stray from the paths and get in among the ancient oaks; craggy old pollards, some living, some dying, some totally moribund – oaken ghosts, sculptural dead wood, insect treasure houses, memorials to the forest's distant past.

The most famous oak tree in the forest is also quite possibly the most famous oak tree in the whole of Britain. The Major Oak stands proudly in the centre of Sherwood Forest; a tree that has been celebrated since 1790 when the local historian Major Hayman Rooke published his *Remarkable Oaks in the Park of Welbeck*, in which he mentions (and provides an illustration of) 'an ancient Oak in Birchland Wood'. Clearly moved by the tree, he remarks: 'I think no one can behold this majestic ruin without pronouncing it to be of very remote antiquity; and might venture to say, that it cannot be much less than a thousand years old.'

Of course by the very nature of its huge, hollow trunk it is very difficult to age, but best estimates today put it at 800 to 1,000 years old, and yet with a girth of 35 feet and a height of 52 feet it's not the biggest or oldest oak in Britain. The tree has long been a local landmark, and was known as the Cockpen Tree in the eighteenth century as its hollow trunk was used as a roost for fighting cocks. In the nineteenth century it became the Major Oak, or Major's Oak, or even the Major, in deference to

The mighty frame of the famous Major Oak - propped, preserved, mulched and fenced in. In May a couple of years back it looked like one of the healthiest ancient oaks in Sherwood. It must be hoped that this great old tree will carry on forever.

Major Hayman Rooke, although it was also sometimes called the Queen or the Queen's Oak, simply reflecting its size or status, as there is no known royal connection. In Edwardian times concerns for the tree's structure led to the first round of chains and braces in the crown and wooden props beneath some of the larger boughs. By the 1970s further concerns were raised about the old tree's health. Huge numbers of visitors were starting to cause compaction problems beneath the tree and undue die-back was starting to occur in the crown. A perimeter fence was erected to keep people at a distance and a bark mulch laid down to encourage worm activity and promote aeration of the root system, with the aim of improving water and nutrient absorption. Putting fences between trees and people can be a little sad, but with more than 600,000 people every year coming from all over the world to see this celebrity maybe it is for the best in this instance.

As the location of the Major Oak suggests, Birchland (Rooke) or Birkland, as this 447-acre remnant of Sherwood is known, was once largely a birch wood growing on heathland. *Birk* is the Viking word for birch. Many of the ancient oaks that are still evident

here could certainly date back 400 to 500 years, which would seem to indicate that a regime of wood pasture prevailed at the time. The antiquarian and historian William Camden, writing in the late sixteenth century, reports upon the ancient Forest of Sherwood or Shirewood as 'anciently thick set with trees, whose entangled branches were so twisted together, that they hardly left room for a single person to pass. At present, it is much thinner, but still breeds an infinite number of deer and stags with lofty antlers.' With plentiful deer in the woods at that time pollards would have been vital if the oaks were to survive. By 1675, the Nottinghamshire historian Robert Thoroton recorded that the forest was 'wonderfully declined' and no doubt this was due to wholesale plundering, both legitimate and illegal, of the best timber trees. Some of the oldest trees still in the forest today are presumably only there because they were deemed of little use for good timber.

As many of the old oaks die, birch is now reclaiming large areas of the forest. Growing, as they do, in light sandy soils, many oaks appear to have been adversely affected by the lowered water table caused by industrial extraction and agricultural drainage

RIGHT One of the craggy old oak pollards in the forest still hangs in there...just.

BELOW An impressive Midland hawthorn on the edge of a clearing with its cascade of May blossom.

and this, combined with the prospect of more frequent periods of drought in coming years, may cause further stress to them. Plans are currently afoot to plant up more oaks in the forest, so one must hope that they fare well. Rowan, hawthorn, holly and the occasional yew make up the rest of the woodland complement here.

Although Sherwood Forest is far more than its single famous denizen, there is a super description by the artist and writer Joseph Rodgers in his late-nineteenth-century *Scenery of Sherwood Forest*, which encapsulates the affection held for the Major Oak:

What memories of happy hours spent in its leafy shade does the name of this tree bring to thousands! Old men in distant cities tell with what pleasure in their youthful days they climbed the Major's great branches, or hid themselves within his hollow trunk; and that when years had sped away and their climbing days were over, these excursions were still remembered as the happiest of the year; and no journey to the forest could ever be made without a call upon the Major, where, reclining on his ancient roots in company with life-long friends, time passed too quickly away.

WHISPERING PINES

GLEN AFFRIC

Caledonian Forest remnant in the Highlands of Scotland

When in Scotland it seems only right that you should experience the splendour of native Scots pine woodland. There are several impressive forests, which are open to the public, where you can steep yourself in the atmosphere of the archetypal Highland habitat; on Deeside there's Glen Tanar and Ballochbuie, on Speyside there's Rothiemurchus and Abernethy, as well as the famous Black Wood of Rannoch in Perthshire. Splendid as they are, few can match the dramatic scenery of Glen Affric, some 20 miles south-west of Inverness, where forest, lochs, river and mountains all come together for the pefect Highland setting.

A Forestry Commission road leads off the public highway, a couple of miles from the village of Cannich, climbing steadily along the hillside above the deep ravine of the River Affric. Look out for a sign for Dog Falls where you can park up and walk alongside the river; the brown, peaty water swirling round roots and boulders before breaking into a deafening roar as it pitches down the deep chasm of the falls. Opportunist birch, emerald in spring, gold in autumn, make a perfect foil for the dark, rugged pines which seem to go on for ever far above you.

Daydream you may, but there's something here that will soon snap you out of your reverie. If this is the first time you've left your car, be it June to September, you will have realized very smartly that you must share this wilderness with the evil Scottish midge. If you're on the move they're not so bad, but as soon as you stop they're upon you; thirsty for blood they will bite you to distraction. Go well prepared with gallons of insect repellent.

The road leads you steadily on up the glen and at times the woods above look impenetrable and forbidding, but, below, a succession of picturesque windows open up across Loch Beinn a' Mheadhain. The sparkling loch with the distant mountains beyond, their lower slopes densely packed with pine and birch, lends a certain perspective to the vista. A sense of euphoria washes over you as you wind further along the glen. At last the woods give way to open ground, where heather, blaeberry, cowberry and bracken carpet the ground, bright green or deep red pillows of moss fill the damper hollows, and small clumps and individual old pines stand in proud isolation. These are the rugged, multi-branched, ruddy-barked veterans of the glen, their crooked forms and knotty boughs of little interest to foresters.

In such a remote spot it seems difficult to believe that most of the forest around you has been cut over several times, particularly during the last 300 years, as timber extraction grew dramatically in the eighteenth century. Travellers and writers into the first half of the nineteenth century often bemoaned the ruinous state of the forests, denuded of the best pines and left as wastelands of brash and stumps, but all was not lost. Landowners needed to replant their pine woods because of the revenue they provided and the cover for game. Often the waste was burnt, which cleared the ground and removed the top layer of peat, thus providing the best gravelly seedbeds for the new generation of pines. Natural forest fires from lightning strikes also helped pine regeneration. However, the potential for this natural regeneration was all but reversed in the late nineteenth century when the priorities for landowners in the Highlands turned to sheep and, of more concern, the encouragement of red deer for hunting. Ever since this period the problem of overgrazing in the pine woods has been a serious obstacle to natural regeneration. Only in recent times has there been a

Early morning view across Loch Beinn a' Mheadhain in Glen Affric, just before an incoming rainstorm lets loose.

concerted effort to fence the deer out to protect the young trees; a process which is now encouraged in regularly changed compartments in order to achieve multi-generational woods.

You should see the red deer in the glen, but they tend to be quite shy, usually staying on high ground until the harsh conditions of winter force them down. In autumn you'll hear them before you see them – those monarchs of the glen roaring and bellowing in rut; gathering their harem about them, warning off the young pretenders and letting everyone know who's the boss round here. There is also a strong possibility that you'll see another highland speciality, the golden eagle, which is Britain's largest raptor, with its remarkable wingspan of around 7 feet, soaring lazily over the mountain, for it prefers the open ground, where it seeks its prey, to the forest. Other special birds to be found among the pines are crossbills, crested tits and the capercaillie. This latter species actually became extinct in the late eighteenth

century due to the loss of habitat as forests were flattened. In the mid-nineteenth century it was reintroduced from Sweden and managed to thrive, and is now widespread. If you're very lucky you may spot a creature that at one time was on the verge of extinction: the pine marten. Almost eradicated in the nineteenth century by gamekeepers and farmers who saw it as a threat to their game-birds and lambs, it was only the diversion of the men with the guns heading off to the fray of the First World War which gave them time and space to rebuild their numbers. They are still rare, but the populations are stable.

It is reputed that the Caledonian Forest once covered 3 million acres, and certainly it was a lot bigger than the vestiges we see today, which amount to a mere 30,000 acres – 1 per cent of the original. However, the pine forests have been in a constant state of flux for thousands of years, due both to climatic changes, that saw huge increases in the blanket bogs where pines wouldn't grow (ancient

An early morning storm blows across Loch Beinn a' Mheadhain.

ABOVE From beneath one of
Glen Affric's majestic pines
Sgurr na Lapaich (3401') can be seen in
the distance still bearing a few patches of
snow in the hollows even in June.

RIGHT Scots pine cones, picked clean of
their nutritious seeds by squirrels,
birds and now by mice and voles, lie
all over the pine forest floor.

remains of the trees are often found beneath the peat), and high levels of human exploitation.

It is debatable whether there is any one place in Scotland with scenery more breathtaking or thoroughly evocative of the ancient Caledonian Forest than Glen Affric. The scale of the place alone, at almost 25,000 acres (a little over 3,500 acres of actual pine forest), is pretty awesome, and a giant highland wilderness such as this almost defies capture with a camera lens. It's that all-encompassing vastness of the landscape; the suggestion of the unseen as well as the seen; the impression of a huge natural forest, much of which has never been tamed or trodden by man (of course this is not true, but it feels like that); the sort of place that makes you feel tiny and insignificant as a human being. Experiencing places like this puts our own existence firmly in perspective. We are right to feel awe-struck, humbled and even responsible for ensuring an unerring future for such wilderness spaces.

THETFORD FOREST

Pines aplenty on the sandy plains of Norfolk

From the outset the enormous scale of Thetford Forest, in the Brecklands of Norfolk, may seem a little daunting; with 46,400 acres to explore, and much of it looking rather similar, you could worry about getting lost here. So, in order to get your bearings, the best bet is to head out of Thetford, towards Brandon, until you reach the Forestry Commission's High Lodge Forest Centre. This is an excellent place to let off steam or simply unwind. As you explore it may be of interest to understand how this landscape has evolved and, latterly, changed into anything but natural. Pine forest it may be, but any comparison to its Caledonian counterpart is purely generic.

Soon after the last Ice Age, during the course of Britain's tree recolonization around 9,500 years ago, native Scots pines were thriving on the thin sandy soils overlying the chalk of East Anglia. Gradually, however, the warming climate pushed the tree's indigenous range ever northwards. Today Scotland is most definitely its native home. Another contributing factor to the disappearance of native pines occurred during the Neolithic period, when East Anglia is thought to have been the most densely populated part of Britain. Wildwood was cleared to make space in order to grow crops, graze livestock, build settlements and of course for fuel. Unlike the broadleaved trees, the pines could not regenerate from the cut stumps, and seedlings were very susceptible to grazing. Although a handful of genuine native Scots pines can still be found in the Brecklands, these are certainly not the 'commercial' pines of Thetford Forest's plantations.

There are still areas of open, flint-strewn heath in the forest – known locally as *brecks* or *breaks*, a term which has persisted since medieval times for tracts of fallow or particularly infertile or unsuitable agricultural land. This enduring characteristic inspired the Norfolk naturalist and historian W.G. Clarke to coin the name Breckland for the region in 1894. The landscape would have changed little over many centuries before the Forestry Commission got weaving with its pine planting in 1922. The majority of the forest today is dominated by dense stands of pine trees, seemingly stretching away to the horizon on every side.

In the early years it was Scots pine that was planted, but not the glorious sub-species *Scotica*, celebrated and admired as the definitive tree of the Caledonian Forest. These plantation pines were sourced from Europe and, in particular, from around Germany's Black Forest, where a strain was known that produced particularly tall, straight trunks – ideal for growing in closely spaced plantations and perfect timber for running through the sawmills. However, they lack the character of *Scotica* with its ruddy, chunky-plated bark and blue-green needles.

The other species with a major presence here is the Corsican pine. Equally as happy as Scots pines on these thin soils, Corsican pine has the added benefit of producing quality timber somewhat faster than its Scots cousin – naturally enough, a boon to profit-seeking foresters. Here and there you will also come upon areas of planted broadleaved trees too, including oak, beech and Roble beech – one of the southern beeches from South America, which seems to do very well in Britain, producing hard, durable timber. There's plenty of birch around too, but that has just blown in naturally, and is only considered a weed by the foresters. Could British forestry be missing a trick here, as birch timber is used in great quantity in Scandinavia for both plywood and superb birch-block flooring? It can also be made into very attractive furniture.

Gerald Wilkinson's *Woodland Walks* book from 1985 provides a remarkable statistic for the use of

As the sun sets across Thetford Forest, the last rays pick out a lone oak which has dared to invade the realm of the Corsican pines.

pine in the mining industry. 'For every 200 tons of coal mined, the Forestry Commission tells us, 1 ton of pinewood props is used – an annual 23,000 cubic metres of peeled logs from Thetford Forest alone.' How times change. One wonders if any timber at all from Thetford finds its way into a coal mine these days.

Thetford Forest is not just a vast space with pines as far as the eye can see, for it has become something of a destination for families seeking an enjoyable, healthy, exciting day out – a high-energy forest. The epicentre is at High Lodge Forest Centre, where you can hire bikes, have a go at orienteering or get the kids exhausted on the Go Ape aerial trekking course

(while you unwind with a gentle stroll, perhaps). There are all kinds of other good things to see here too, as Thetford Forest Park actually includes seventeen different sites. To the north there's Lynford Arboretum, with more than 200 different species of trees, and Lynford Lakes, which is a great place for birdwatchers, with kingfisher, crossbill and hawfinch all in evidence. You'll notice the name 'warren' turns up repeatedly in these parts, and this is because from medieval times onwards rabbit warrens were kept by each landowner as a ready source of fresh meat for the table. They had warreners too, who were employed to keep the rabbits in and the poachers out. Shouldham Warren is an outlying site to the

Thetford Forest is dominated by pines – mainly Scots and Corsican, but they can have a particularly dramatic effect in the right light.

north-west, Mildenhall Warren is to the south-west and several compartments of the core forest are also warrens.

Between Thetford and Swaffham it is well worth exploring some of the minor roads to discover a landscape feature which is most peculiar and exclusive to this part of Britain, namely the pine rows or 'deal rows' (deal being the local name for all conifers). Head for Cockley Cley, where all the roads radiating out from the village are lined with old Scots pines which are bent and twisted, sometimes like giant arboreal corkscrews. In the late eighteenth century local landowners thought that they could make hedges and windbreaks out of the pines, mainly to stop the wind whipping all the topsoil off their land. It's patently obvious now that the pines weren't ever going to play the traditional role of hedge tree, and by the late nineteenth century the whole idea had been abandoned. Slowly but surely the laid pines unwound and rose up to become the strange and beautiful forms they are today.

ABOVE A typical track across the forest. On the left, young Corsican pines grow around a landmark Austrian pine, left from a previous crop. On the right, the golden autumn show of southern beech.

LEFT At Cockley Cley, just south of Swaffham, one of the bizarre 'deal rows' of contorted Scots pines lines a roadside verge.

WOODS IN HIGH PLACES

GLEN FINGLAS

A wealth of veteran trees and awesome vistas in the Loch Lomond and Trossachs National Park

The first thing that strikes you as you walk along the track that leads into Glen Finglas is the sheer scale of the place, at almost 12,000 acres it does look a vast space; and it's a space that leads your eye to the horizon almost every way you look. The Glen Finglas Estate seems to encapsulate all that is best about the wilderness landscapes of Scotland; laid out before you the sweeping glen stretches into the distance, beyond the shimmering waters of the reservoir, with the gentle hump of Meall Cala centre stage. Apart from a few grazing sheep or cattle this wide-open landscape may seem barren and lifeless. Nothing could be further from the truth.

Glen Finglas, and its tributary glens to the east – Glen Meann and Glen Casaig – has a long and colourful history as a royal hunting forest, particularly between the early fourteenth century and the eighteenth century, when a succession of Scottish kings and earls came regularly to hunt. James II even built a hunting lodge in the glen. Like so many Scottish forests, it dispels that popular notion of a forest being heavily wooded. The forest was a place of deer rather than trees, and the red deer still roam free here. For the last 200 years the glen has largely been used as grazing for livestock, but this, coupled with an over abundance of deer, has not always been in the best interests of the trees.

The romance of these wild Scottish landscapes appealed greatly to the Victorians and Glen Finglas was very firmly on many people's itinerary. John Ruskin visited often; his most famous portrait by Sir John Everett Millais in 1853 shows Ruskin standing by the river at Brig o' Turk. Sir Walter Scott also drew inspiration for his epic poem *The Lady of the Lake* and a ballad about a fatal hunting expedition entitled *Glenfinlas*.

In 1996 a new departure was launched for Glen Finglas when the estate was purchased by the Woodland Trust, with help from the Heritage Lottery Fund. The glen is now the largest site owned by the Trust, and represents a massive project for conservation and regeneration. Heralding itself as 'Keeper of the Forest', the Trust aims to enhance the ancient woodland and devise a sustainable balance between people and this very special landscape.

There is splendour here at any time of year: late summer with the purple heather at its best and scarlet clusters of fruit decking the rowans; the array of yellows, golds and browns in autumn, the red stags barking and bellowing on the hills; come winter and the snow blows in, picking out the contours and the stark, relief forms of the ancient trees. In spring the glen refreshes, the burns gurgle with mountain-top melt waters, the vibrant greens return to the trees and a new generation of flowers speckle the upland turf.

Compared to many parts of Britain, spring comes relatively late to these upland realms. A walk in late May or June finds the trees in full leaf. In the upper parts of the glens there is a mixture of woodland, which tends to follow the wetter flushes or the numerous burns and margins of the rivers in the bottom. Glen Finglas itself is the best endowed with veteran trees, many of which are ancient – in some cases the oldest alders may be up to 400 years old. The dominant species are undoubtedly birch and alder, with a very small complement of sessile oak, hazel, rowan and ash as well as dwarf willows on the wetter heath areas.

However, it's the historic management of this upland wood that makes it so special, for this is wood pasture, defined by an assemblage of veteran alders, most of which have been harvested in the

A lone downy birch at the top of Glen Finglas, bent and bowed by the wind, but still thriving.

Lichens are everywhere in the crystal clear air of the glen and this 'micro-landscape' of lichens covers just a few square inches of a boulder.

OPPOSITE

TOP A splendid hoary old birch pollard above the reservoir. It's anyone's guess as to when this tree was last pollarded.

BOTTOM Sometimes the 'cuckoo' rowans that grow within the ancient alders in Glen Finglas appear to have fused themselves together, as in this example poised above the river.

the trees within trees. Rowan berries, dropped long ago by some visiting bird in the fork of an old alder pollard, germinated in the detritus, miraculously found enough sustenance to keep going, somehow pushed a root system down through the rotting or hollow heart of the alder, and just grew and grew. The result, decades if not over a century later, is that extremely large rowan trees flourish within alders … and it's not just the odd tree – there are dozens of them. Sometimes the two species seem almost fused together. Sometimes the rowan has grown so large that it has burst the old alder apart, emerging like something from *The Alien*; occasionally you can see down into the shell of the alder and pick out the aerial roots of the rowan.

When you get up to the higher reaches of Glen Finglas it's good to stop and sit and take in the scene about you; the peace only broken by the bleating of Blackface sheep or the tuneful twitter of skylarks. The classic U shape before you is indelibly of glacial origin. Most of the land is given over to a mixture of acid grassland, marsh and heath and, remarkably, only 6 per cent of what you view is woodland. The Woodland Trust is on a mission to redress the balance. It has fenced off compartments of woodland to encourage natural regeneration; it is busily planting native broadleaved trees and Scots pine; and, among the old pollards in the revived wood-pasture regime, its sheep and Luing cattle have been retained to maintain the heath and grassland through grazing. Both red and roe deer are usually in the glen, but seldom in sufficient numbers to cause significant damage to trees. It's a sensitive job to get right, but with plenty of fine-tuning and adaptation future prospects look good.

When so much of the British countryside still strives to shut people out, to maintain unreasonable, unnecessary privacy, how cheering and positive that in Scotland every bit of the great outdoors is accessible to one and all. Moreover, the Woodland Trust extends a warm welcome to this stunning estate, recognized as one of its flagship sites. Glen Finglas, or Gleann Fionnghlais to credit its Gaelic name properly, means 'Glen of the white water' or 'Fair and green glen'. Either will do very nicely.

past as high-cut coppice stools or pollards; this was a working landscape where trees in open ground had to co-exist with grazing animals. This regime probably petered out during the nineteenth century, when the population here started to decrease significantly, but it has left a legacy of veteran trees, rich in character and hugely important in terms of habitat. The downy birch were cut over too, and some of these trees, bearing their deeply fissured bark, have become veritable gardens for mosses and lichens. In fact more than 80 different lichens have been recorded here. And yet, as you ramble through the glen, it will be the alders to which you are constantly drawn, for seldom do you see alders growing like this anywhere else in Britain – at least not so many of them in one place.

It's the forms that fascinate. Some trees have dropped boughs that have then layered themselves and grown up again. Others have fallen in storms, but then carried on growing horizontally, sometimes the boughs on top of the trunk developing into great girthed trees in their own right. Strangest of all are

HIGH SHORES CLOUGH WOOD

Woodland retreat with commanding views of the Manchester conurbation

You know you're in northern territories when you encounter the 'clough' appellation. The word is derived from the Anglo-Saxon *cleofian* indicating a breach, cleave or divide, and now frequently appertaining to a small or narrow valley in the landscape, particularly in northern England. High Shores Clough Wood is faithful to the description. It actually consists of two converging cloughs, which cut down from the moor edge above the leafy northern suburbs of Bolton, Lancashire.

Leaving the busy northern ringroad near Moss Bank Park, the journey towards the wood leads you up through a changed and gentrified valley. More than a century ago vast mills rattled and roared at the peak of the cotton industry. Today the mills have gone, all is peaceful, and the mill owners' fine houses and rows of mill workers' cottages are now character period homes. The Dean Brook still splashes merrily along the valley bottom, yet its power potential for industry is a thing of the past. A lasting memorial to all this activity in the valley survives as the soaring 260-foot chimney of the erstwhile Smithills Bleach Works. The chimney is also a fitting tribute to the native Boltonian, celebrity steeplejack and all-round character Fred Dibnah, who not only carried out repair work to it but was also instrumental in getting it a Grade 2 listing.

Near a fine stone bridge, which swings the narrow lane over the river and steeply up the hill, you will find the lower entrance to the wood. A circular walk takes in all the aspects that make High Shores Clough so special and yet so typical. In the valley bottom you can feel quite hemmed in, the steep sides being virtually impossible to scale in places. As one might expect in these acidic uplands, the main components here are sessile oak and birch, with alder in the wetter flushes and along the river banks. Beech has clearly been introduced in the distant past

and, of course, sycamore has insinuated itself here with its usual vigour. Love it or loathe it, sycamore has a long history of success throughout the north of Britain and has made a massive contribution to the treescape. It may be a major element of some woods, but is seldom the dominant species. It is a brilliant shade tree, makes excellent shelter belts for homesteads and provides fine timber.

Perhaps less welcome along the water's edge are clumps of Japanese knotweed – officially designated as Britain's most pernicious weed, its ability to colonize quite awesome. Originally introduced around 1830 as a garden plant in London, nobody could have guessed quite how successful its march across Britain would be. It is now to be found the length and breadth of the country. The distinctive pungent smell of Himalayan balsam – another highly successful interloper from afar – also hangs in the still air of the valley. The exotic pink flowers are extremely pretty, but when you've seen the catapulted seeds flying from the ripened seedpods, arcing to some fresh, fallow spot, you instantly realize the reproductive potential of this plant too. The vegetation might be considered a little austere in these upland woods and so, perhaps in moderation, these aliens bring variety to the scene; and yet it would be tragic if they reach saturation levels to the point of excluding the native flora.

To get the best sense of this upland wood you need to get to the top, and the fastest way to get there is up the dead-straight flight of sixty-three beautifully dressed stone steps, once the route taken to the moors by the miners and quarrymen of old. Health and safety appears to have decreed that these should have metal railings up either side. They look a little incongruous, but if it helps those who are less able and makes the steps safer for children so be it. When you hit the top of the hill as often as

In the bottom of High Shores Clough Wood, where peaty waters gurgle down from the moors above through woods of oak, beech and sycamore.

LEFT The sweet, musky sent of Indian or Himalayan balsam pervades the valley bottom, as this introduced plant has insinuated itself all along the damp margins of the river. First introduced as a garden plant in 1839, it is now naturalised all over Britain, to the point where it is often out of control and regarded as a weed. To watch the explosive pods jettison their seeds soon makes you realise why it has been so successful. However, because of its exotic flowers it is sometimes known as 'poor man's orchid'.

BELOW In early winter the silky, silvery stems of birch catch the late afternoon sunlight on the moors above the wood.

A view from the moors above High Shores Clough Wood, south across nearby Bolton and further on to the Manchester conurbation.

not a stiff breeze fills your lungs. You can tell this moor is wild and woolly for the wiry moor grasses are bent double, and the silver birches on the upper edge of the woodland have been whipped clean of their autumn leaves long before their fellows tucked in the shelter of the valleys. A handful of hardy but wary sheep observe your slow progress across the windswept moor.

Once clear of the wood edge, you turn to view your surroundings, staring back across an impressive panorama dominated, to the south, nearby Bolton and beyond the vast sprawl of the Manchester conurbation. There's a certain pleasure to be derived, standing dreaming on a remote hill, feeling like an escapee from the cut and thrust of that distant city life. On the moorside around you austere gritstone farms and barns squat squarely in the barren landscape, their ground clearly delineated by networks of drystone walls or threadbare hedgerows of gnarled old hawthorns and, where little else would dare to grow, a few clumps of steadfast sycamores protect the farmsteads and haggard pines scrape the skyline.

For some people, more used to the lush lowland woods of southern England, landscapes like this may appear too spartan, but for those with northern roots (among whom I count myself) and those who live here, these modest clough woodlands have long been a breath of fresh air.

HEARTS OF OAK

THE LOCHWOOD OAKS

A long–neglected wood pasture in the Scottish Borders with a fascinating modern purpose

Oak is certainly the most widespread native broadleaf of British woods – whether as dominant or contributing species, the common and the sessile oak between them are the stereotypical if not iconic woodland trees. Their forms may vary according to location, soil type or their history of human management, but oak is the most instantly recognizable.

In Scotland there is a long history of intensive oak-wood management, which means that the vast majority of such woods have been coppiced in the past to provide fuel wood, charcoal or tan bark, leaving most of them rather devoid of particularly large oak trees, unless they were old standards or pollards that were poorly formed and not deemed worthy of felling for timber. Modern, planted oak woods have tended to be coppice-with-standard regimes, or single-generation plantations of relatively little visual interest and often limited biodiversity. Popular thinking at present is aiming to encourage multi-generational oak (or mixed broadleaf) woods, ideally through natural regeneration or, where necessary, aided by selective felling and planting. Ultimately, it is hoped, this near-natural woodland regeneration will provide broader habitat scope for flora and fauna. Since the nineteenth century various authorities have proposed natural regeneration, but it is fraught with problems. Small rodents eat the acorns, moth larvae strip leaves, deer or sheep eat seedlings, competing ground cover may stifle seedlings and the shade of dense woodland canopy restricts light levels. So if this regime is to succeed a little human assistance is usually required.

A few very singular sites in Scotland have developed, largely through neglect rather than by active management, into oak woods with a decidedly ancient character. However, one of the finest examples is Lochwood Oaks, near Moffat, in Dumfries &

Galloway. In the shadow of Lochwood Tower, the ruinous residence of the Clan Johnstone, lies an oak wood of a most extraordinary nature. A glorious community of knobbly, veteran sessile oak pollards, bedecked with mosses, lichens and ferns, crouch amid a sea of bracken. The wood is a combination of the kind of ancient oaks that you might expect to find in a forest such as Sherwood, or a deer park such as Windsor, combined with the rich bryophyte colonies you would see in the Atlantic oak woods of the west coast. The only reason that these trees have survived so long is because they were pollarded over hundreds of years in a wood-pasture regime.

Their story may be obscure, for there is little historic information available, but the presence of nearby Lochwood Tower may offer clues. The first mention of the house is in 1476, so a mid- to late-fifteenth-century building date has been assumed. As the main residence of the Johnstones, it appears to have had a precarious existence, being captured by the English in 1547, who promptly burned it down as they left in 1550. Rebuilt, it was yet again burned down in 1585 by the rival Maxwell family. The castle was rebuilt once more, but by the early eighteenth century must have been considered outmoded, for it was then abandoned by the Earl of Annandale. The proximity of the wood with its pollards would seem to indicate a small deer park or at least some sort of enclosure where animals grazed. The Reverend Dr John Walker writes of the wood in his *Essays* in 1773 and again, in 1836, John James Hope-Johnstone, 7th Earl of Annandale and Hartfell, corresponds with the horticulturalist J.C. Loudon about the largest oak in the wood: 'This tree stands in a wood of oaks, in which the Castle of Lochwood

One of the largest ancient oaks at Lochwood, cloaked in mosses, lichens and polypody ferns, stands amid the wind tossed bracken.

(the original residence of the Johnstone family) is situated. It is quite vigorous; but most of the other trees are in a state of decay.' The nineteenth-century ornithologist, botanist and artist Prideaux John Selby also briefly mentions Lockwood (sic) in 1842. A reasonable guesstimate of the age of some of the older oaks would be in the 400–500-year range. However, in fairly recent times that guess has been converted into hard fact.

In the mid-1970s Lochwood was chosen, as one of a very select group of sites in Scotland, for a study of annual growth rings, otherwise known as dendrochronology. Every year a tree lays down a new layer of cambium, which shows as an annual ring. Depending upon the prevailing climatic conditions, these rings may be narrow in unfavourable years (particularly drought) and wider in favourable ones. Each ring consists of a less dense and more dense layer of cells, which corresponds to the spring and summer growth, the contrasting light and dark tones making each annual ring discernible. In 1973 and 1975 Dr Mike Baillie, from Queen's University Belfast, took core samples from the oaks at Lochwood, and

by cross-matching sixteen of them he obtained a chronology for the site, which established a range from 1571 to 1975. By 1977 this study, along with others in lowland Scotland and Northern Ireland, as well as core samples from a variety of timbers from historic buildings, built a master chronology that extended from AD946–1975. Subsequently, over the last thirty years, with access to even older timber artefacts and bog oak, this chronology has been extended to 7,000 years. In practicality, a spread of annual rings in a piece of oak timber can now be matched to some point along this master map to establish age and, if there is the presence of sapwood, a felling date can be verified too. This information is of huge significance to archaeologists, architects, conservators and climatologists and it has also provided an invaluable cross-reference for carbon-dating.

There has been a long recent history of an unfenced, open aspect to Lochwood which must have put any natural regeneration of the oaks under serious pressure, what with roe and fallow deer in abundance, and probably grazing sheep and cattle

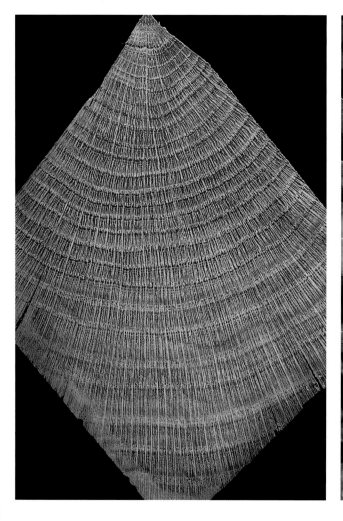

LEFT This old piece of oak timber salvaged during the restoration of my house shows about 30 annual rings, with the core of the tree at the top point. The widest rings are about 10mm – exceptional, but not uncommon during the early years of growth. In order to date a piece of timber by dendrochronology at least 60 growth rings are required, and preferably 120, and presence of sapwood will provide a felling date for the tree.

RIGHT Sessile oaks are easily identified by the stemless acorns which sit snugly on the twig.

A glorious burry, whiskery old oak leans off a boundary bank at the bottom of Lochwood. Fortunately the conifer plantation beyond stopped short of enveloping the ancient oaks.

in the past as well. Recently, deer fences have been erected around a large section of the wood, so it will be interesting to see what happens on the woodland floor. Spaces for sunlight to penetrate are there, although some bracken control will probably have to be instigated to open up the ground for young trees.

It is actually very fortunate that the oaks have survived so well here, since beech wood is encroaching from the northern end and stands of conifer forestry overlap with the woodland margins. Its continuing survival is a testament to the great good sense of the present Earl of Annandale. You can admire the wood from the narrow lane which weaves through it. Simply to stand among these grand old trees, wondering by whom and exactly when they were last pollarded, imagining the sights they've witnessed over the last 450 years or more in this turbulent border region, is an unforgettable experience.

HELMETH WOOD

Splendid oak coppice wood among the Stretton Hills of Shropshire

The monumental task of selecting a typical oak wood from among the many thousands of oak-dominated woods around Britain is truly daunting; and, after all, there are so many different oak woods that the epithet 'typical' soon becomes redundant. Everyone will have their own particular favourites. Some people will be influenced by personal associations – their local wood, part of a long-familiar landscape, great for walking the dog, memories of childhood rambles or building dens with their mates. Some will recall badger watching or catching a fleeting glimpse of a deer. Others will be lured by wild flowers or birdlife or the infinite variety of bugs and beasties. Oaks do, after all, have a greater diversity of insect life associated with them than most other tree species. Almost wherever you live in Britain there will be some ramification of an oak wood within striking distance.

There's something very special about the oak, albeit we have two native species – the English, common or pedunculate oak is the broad, spreading tree of the lowlands while the durmast or sessile is essentially the oak of uplands and acidic soils. Whichever it may be, the oak is undoubtedly Britain's tree icon – inextricably part of our landscape, history and national culture since ancient times; from the sacred groves of the Druids in pre-Christianity to the tree of choice for ceremonial and celebratory planting today.

British oak woods survive in the modern landscape largely because they have traditionally been woods of utility – a valuable resource; providing communities with construction timber and fuel wood as well as providing landowners with revenue from charcoal, tan bark or large-scale timber for buildings or shipbuilding. For centuries oak woods were the source of gainful employment, not just for the woodsmen who worked within them, but also for all the artisans who used the timber that the woodland produced. Many local economies were reliant on their oak woods, while further afield industries such as leather manufacturing and iron smelting were equally dependent. Most of the ancient oak woods today bear all the signs of historic exploitation, and yet few of them are now intensively managed.

As my own example of a 'typical' oak wood I have chosen Helmeth Wood, a 59-acre woodland in the heart of the Shropshire Hills Area of Outstanding Natural Beauty, overlooking the little market town of Church Stretton. Helmeth Hill is part of the long broken ridge of hills to the east of the town and, although not as immediately popular with tourists who usually tend to head west for Cardingmill Valley or beyond to the Long Mynd, there's plenty of good walking, with cracking views and often peace and solitude as a bonus. The Precambrian Uriconian rock from which this ridge was formed was pushed up by volcanic action many millions of years ago; an evolution vividly credible as you approach from a distance or as you negotiate the craggy tops.

Viewing Helmeth Hill and the wooded swathes of its slopes from nearby Hope Bowdler Hill gives the strong impression of a remnant from a once widely wooded landscape, which avoided clearance for pasture several hundred years ago. Here the contrast is marked between the gentle lower slopes, where it was feasible to carve out land with agricultural potential, and the steep upper slopes that were left wooded; the obvious practicalities of hauling timber downhill from the wood also making a lot of sense.

Inside Helmeth it soon becomes apparent that this is quite an even aged wood. Records reveal that about ninety years ago, during the First World

A winter's morning in pastures below Helmeth Wood. The fine field oak almost seems to have slid down the hill out of the wood.

War, most of it was cut over for timber and coppice wood. This has left many impressive old sessile oaks, which are outgrown coppice stools with several large trunks. Birch, ash and alder are also major elements of this wood, and the presence of small-leaved lime, along with spring flowers such as yellow archangel, bluebells and wood sorrel, help to establish Helmeth's ancient credentials.

Several paths wind through the wood and, although it's a fairly stiff climb to the summit, the glimpses out across the adjacent landscape make it all worthwhile. To create more diversity and interest, the Woodland Trust has plans in hand to cordon off regeneration coupes, which will exclude deer and give young trees a chance to thrive. It will also instigate some selective thinning in the wood, thus opening up glades to encourage natural regeneration on the woodland

ABOVE View west from Hope Bowdler Hill across Helmeth Wood towards Church Stretton and the Stretton Hills beyond. Ancient hawthorns and birches sit astride the old field boundary in the foreground.

RIGHT Wood sorrel is a delightful little plant of ancient woodland. Perhaps known more for its trefoil, shamrock-shaped leaves it does bear this particularly delicate little flower. The plant grows happily in shady places and may sometimes be found in the aerial hollows of trees.

Old oak coppice stools on a wintry morning.

floor and attract more butterflies. Every effort will be made to leave plenty of dead wood too, thus boosting invertebrate populations.

When snowfall is fast becoming a rare occurrence in lowland England, I ventured to Helmeth last winter and found a wood very different from the Helmeth of the previous spring. Any wood in early May, crammed with bluebells, can draw you in with its seductive scent and carpet of blue; the busy chatter and bustle of nesting birds all around you. In winter all is silent. All is monochromatic. The wood is mute; muffled by a thin blanket of snow. Yet it's still very much alive, appearing to hold its breath; the life-forces poised beneath the earth. The crisp rustle of frozen oak leaves underfoot and the occasional dull thud of snow falling from a bough are all that break the chilled silence.

Is this wood a typical oak wood? Who has the right to define it thus? All oak woods are special; particularly those with an ancient lineage, and every one of them will have something that makes them unique. The geographical location, the terrain, the history, the management, the flora and fauna they support, and quite simply every individual's experience of oak woods will be different. Depending on what time of day, the weather or the season you visit, Britain's vast array of oak woods offers limitless fascination for those who care to explore them.

ATLANTIC RAINFORESTS

NANT GWYNANT

A rich and rugged woodland in the shadow of Snowdon

Nant Gwynant is the valley or pass that runs to the north-east of Beddgelert, one of Snowdonia's key centres for the thousands of visitors who regularly sample the delights of high-level walking in the area. One of the most popular routes up to the summit of Snowdon is the famous Watkin Path – a stunningly beautiful ascent which originates from the Bethania car park, between Llyn Dinas and Llyn Gwynant. How often, in their great haste to get on to the mountain proper, must walkers have swiftly traversed the lower reaches of the fine oak woods here with barely a thought for the rest of this very special wood sweeping away up the rocky slopes.

Although these woods, immediately to the west of the road, do not appear to be named as such, they are a relic of what one suspects was once a far more widespread woodland type in this north-west corner of Wales. Known to woodland experts as the Atlantics, these are wet oak woods, with sheltered hollows and ravines, endowed with rich colonies of mosses, liverworts and lichens, which bedeck trees and boulders alike. Some authorities have suggested that these western oak woods might have been sheltered and warm enough (thanks to the Gulf Stream) to have remained free of ice during the last Ice Age and thus you may be observing a woodland flora that has evolved for many thousands, if not millions of years.

Several seldom trodden, narrow paths weave uphill from the base of the wood. The oaks are constant companions; venerable and crooked, their size belies their age. They often grow from rocky clefts in the crags or among the clutter of giant mossy boulders. Trees grow very slowly in these upland realms, but

OPPOSITE Early-morning view along Llyn Gwynant, with Nant Gwynant and Yr Aran in the distance.

LEFT Oaks dominate the steep boulder-strewn slopes of the wood.

LEFT Autumnal beeches in the lower reaches of the wood.

OPPOSITE The view eastward over Nant Gwynant with Llyn Gwynant and Carnedd y Cribau in the distance. A day to relish among the mountains of Snowdonia.

many have been coppiced in the past so they don't really reflect the true antiquity of what you see today. Where oak doesn't grow the opportunist birch has taken hold, and many are rugged old trees with deeply furrowed bark. In the middle of the upper reaches of the wood a long-neglected beech plantation has escaped from old pollard management into towering multi-stemmed trees. Some are thriving, while others have reached their allotted span, gradually collapsing and rotting away. Some have clearly succumbed to storms; splintered and rent asunder, their old grey limbs lean and lie about the woodland floor, creating dead-wood havens for invertebrates galore and plinths for delicate processions of fungi. Where trees fall sylvan vignettes of the valley below open up, but the thought of finding the very best views drives you further uphill, beyond the highest fringes of the wood and on to the open mountainside.

Here, a few oaks have escaped the wood's perimeter stone wall, the wind sculpting their profiles. Some are flat-topped mushroomesque forms; others simply moulded in tune with the undulations of the hillside about them. Above the nearby gurgling stream, a few odd, exposed rowans stand out against the sky. Probably sprung from washed-down berries, their own vermilion fruits tumble with the current to some other random nook or cranny to begin another round. The view east, out along the valley, is well worth the short scramble out of the wood. Llyn Gwynant sparkles in the distance and beyond the perfect peak of Carnedd y Cribau points sharply

aloft. To the north the foothills of Snowdon, below Y Lliwedd; to the south the conifer-bound tump of Coederyr. On a sunny day in spring or autumn, with clouds chasing each other in an azure sky, while their errant shadows scud in mirror image across the mountains, you may suspect that you've found a little piece of heaven here.

Back inside the wood there are a few little promontories on the hillside which lead you out to some other good views. At one viewpoint you can look northwards, up into Cwm Llam, and see the very tip of Snowdon peeking out above the foothills. It looks a lot more than 3,000 feet above. A few aliens have done their best to infiltrate – sycamore has found gaps to colonize and the dreaded rhododendron is doing its best to get a toehold. The National Trust will have to be vigilant or this pink-flowered pest could wreck the wonderful balance of such a wood.

On my way out of the trees, lost in my own thoughts, I rounded the base of a large boulder and came face to face with a very small, but quite fearsome-looking billy-goat. We sized each other up for what seemed like an eternity. He snorted a little contemptuously and resumed his grazing. I, somewhat relieved, gave him a wide berth, and trudged off out of the wood with the strong whiff of goat musk wafting after me. In his wake I spied his harem, who never even gave me a second glance. I assume they are in there as part of some grazing regime, but, equally, feral goats are known to frequent many Snowdonia woods. Either way, it would have been nice to know.

SUNART OAK WOODS

Wet wild woods, clad in lichen and fern, on Scotland's west coast

The deep inlet of the sea loch of Sunart, to the south-west of Fort William, funnels warm currents from the passing Gulf Stream along the southern shores of the Ardnamurchan Peninsula, on Scotland's west coast. The mild, unpolluted climate and an abundance of rain make the perfect conditions for fantastic oak woods, dripping with ferns, mosses, liverworts and lichens. Atlantic woods occur sporadically along the west coast of Britain, but the Scottish examples in particular are some of the most remote and imbue an overwhelming atmosphere of a primeval landscape. The term Atlantic is usually ascribed to the period between 5500BC and 3000BC, when Britain's climate warmed but also became much wetter, and conditions are pretty much the same today in these westerly oak woods.

The majority of the oaks, both sessile and pedunculate, in these woods are relatively small. Their growth rate has been modest on the thin and rockbound acid soils and they have also long been subjected to a regular round of coppicing. What they lack in size they can more than compensate for in density, where seemingly impenetrable woods dominate some of the steeper slopes above the loch side. Even when struggling through dense bracken beneath the oaks you may come upon remnants of ancient habitations or long-forgotten trackways, suggesting that when the woods were more actively managed there were lots more people living here and frequently traversing the wooded areas – either extracting firewood, timber or tan bark, burning charcoal or perhaps driving livestock from one pasture to another. There is evidence of different kinds of woodland management in the past, with both coppice woods and the remnants of wood pasture, containing old pollards, still to be seen.

Fortunately for Sunart and its very special woodlands the establishment of the Sunart Oakwoods Initiative in 1996, whereby several agencies and the local communities came together with the common aim of enhancing and expanding the native woodland, has been a great success. With an eye to conservation, local economy and amenity, incorporating greater access and boosting local tourism, the stewards of this initiative are successfully addressing the whole panoply of issues to keep the future of the region's wildlife and communities as one interdependent, vibrant force.

The native oak woods are now carefully protected against alien invasion or wholesale removal for commercial forestry. The oaks share their woods with ash, rowan, downy birch, hazel, holly and wych elm with plenty of alder in the wetter areas. More than 300 different species of mosses and liverworts, and over 200 different lichens luxuriate in the constantly damp conditions, colonizing virtually every tree – different species favouring particular locations. The sun-seeking, more drought-resistant species will be happy on the southern and western aspects, while those requiring more shade and moisture colonize the northern sides of the tree boles; some so densely that it often becomes difficult to pick out any tree bark at all.

The woods in early spring are a haven for primroses and wood anemones, closely followed by bluebells, but Sunart is also renowned for its many orchids, the rarest being two Red Data Book species: Irish lady's tresses and Pugsley's marsh orchid (known locally as Lapland marsh orchid). Most butterflies have very particular affinities to certain conditions and food plants, and the chequered skipper, until the Second World War a common species throughout Britain, is now restricted to north-west Scotland, Sunart being one of its strongholds.

Alien influences have come into play along Ardnamurchan over the last century affecting the

In the damper defiles of the Sunart oak woods the mosses, lichens and ferns are at their most luxuriant.

The wind whips through the dense ground cover of bracken beneath the oaks on the north shore of Loch Sunart.

native woodland. High demand for more softwood timber saw vast tracts of land taken for conifer plantations – a trend which has been stabilized, if not reversed in recent times. However, the habitat value to some species, typically red squirrels, of conifer woods must still be acknowledged. The injudicious introduction of the rhododendron during the eighteenth and nineteenth centuries, once deemed a useful and handsome shrub for beautifying some of the large estates, has resulted in a plant that is out of control. Eradication programmes are now under way to halt this pernicious weed before it squeezes out everything else. Other shrubs and ground flora are suppressed beneath its deep shade and the total lack of sunlight means that natural regeneration of tree seedlings is also well-nigh impossible. Without slash and burn techniques, followed up with chemical control, the tenacious root systems spring anew with Hydra-like intensity. The dark, leathery leaves are toxic, which makes them unpalatable for animals.

That said, as the innocent tourist drives along the peninsula, it's very hard not to be impressed by the massed ranks of rhododendron with their exotic deep pink blooms.

The wildlife of Sunart is memorable. Great herds of red and roe deer roam the hillsides, and pine martens and wildcats thrive here. The impressive spans of golden eagles and white-tailed eagles can also be spotted wheeling lazily, far above. With patience you'll spy red squirrels scampering among the trees, but they are usually much shyer than their grey American cousins, which, thankfully, have not arrived here . . . yet. It is an ongoing fascination to many that red squirrels appear to thrive in the native oak woods here, as it is widely believed that their main food source and usual habitat is among conifers (of which there are usually spruce, larch or pine not far away). None the less the squirrels are finding enough sustenance among the oaks.

RIGHT An oak anchored in a rocky cleft on the foreshore has grown two boughs which have strangely grafted themselves together in a circle – a process known as inarching. Where the tree emerges the face of a great rock fish appears.

BELOW Without doubt the rhododendron is a beautiful and exotic-looking shrub when in flower, but its rampant colonization at the expense of virtually any other plant in its path has proved problematic both here and in many other parts of Britain.

If you are even luckier there is a slim chance of watching otters pottering about the shoreline of the loch. Some thirty-five years ago I was fortunate enough to meet up with one of the local estate gamekeepers who was well acquainted with the otters' usual haunts. One evening we crept down through the woods to within 200 yards of the loch and sat and waited . . . and waited and just as we thought nature was ignoring our patience and fortitude (the midges were no joke) a female otter emerged into the shallows with two almost mature pups at her heels. We held our breath, watching, captivated as she dragged a large fish on to the rocks. She appeared to tease the pups for a while, letting them steal it from her and then snatching it back, before it became their plaything and finally a meal. What a privilege to see these stunning creatures in the wild. Such experiences stay with you all your life.

BELOW Low morning sunlight gilds the boughs of oaks in the bottom of the wood.

OPPOSITE Morning sunlight glances across the bared winter boughs of oaks along the West Looe river.

DOWN TO THE SEA

KILMINORTH WOOD

Billowing oaks above the West Looe Estuary in Cornwall

Many of the river estuaries along the south coast of Cornwall do have a certain similarity, as so often their dense, oak-dominant woods which shroud the valley sides plunge like great arboreal Brillo pads from the pastures on the hilltops to hover precariously above the high-tide mark. A few of these oaks have their roots well and truly submerged in brackish tidal mud and they are doing extremely well.

The bustling little town of Looe, very popular with holiday-makers, judging by its mammoth car park, straddles the estuary just below the confluence of the East and West Looe rivers, its bright rows of compact cottages stepping away up every available inch of hillside. The drive down to Looe hugs the East Looe river for the last couple of miles, giving you ample chance to get the feel of the woodland hereabouts. Park up in Caradon District Council's vast car park and you are at the very gateway into Kilminorth Wood.

An early-morning expedition is a good choice, as the rising sun runs up the West Looe river gilding the treetops as the woods on the north side of the river become a burnished filigree of twisted and contorted oak boughs. At low tide you may spot curlews or dunlin sifting the mud for tasty morsels. At high tide there's a chance of seeing the piercing, iridescent blue flash of a hunting kingfisher and the riverside is also the haunt of those startlingly bright-white little egrets. One of Britain's most recent colonizers, egrets have moved in from Europe over the last twenty years and now appear at many sites along the south coast. The RSPB estimates that around 150 breeding pairs are resident and as many as 1,600 birds overwinter here. When you see one the first thought is that it may be a small albino heron – understandable, as they are of the same family. Herons, of course, are here too and, as you walk the edge of the river, you can spot shelduck and redshank.

One of the larger oak coppice stools in the bottom of the wood blends with the rocky bank from which it grows, accompanied by an understorey of holly, which is so typical of these woods.

Autumn turns to winter along the West Looe river, where Kilminorth Wood (on the left) reaches right down to the shoreline. The white dot in the distance is a little egret.

Because so many people love to use this wood you will need to plan your visit outside weekends or the early-morning and after-work dog-exercising periods if you want to quietly catch up on the wildlife of Kilminorth. The birdlife is always good, but there are also chances to see badgers, foxes, deer; and with luck and patience you may find dormice and, along the river margins, otters.

Kilminorth is ancient woodland, the tree cover rising up above principally sessile oak wood with an understorey largely of holly and hazel. Some of the oldest oaks in the wood are to be found along the river's edge – glorious, burry old coppice stools full of deep, dark hollows, with impressive roots which stubbornly anchor them to the constantly undercut river bank. The acidic nature of the soil encourages heather, blaeberry and the delicate common cow-wheat, an annual with tiny lemon-yellow flowers, which is a good ancient woodland indicator plant. The bluebells in spring are a wonderful sight, and Kilminorth is also renowned for its lichens, mosses and ferns. Downy birch and ash spring up when gaps open in the wood, and alder and grey willow seem to like the lower, wetter slopes. Introduced trees include sweet chestnut, beech and sycamore, the latter being closely monitored to prevent it crowding out indigenous species.

Until recently there had been little management inside the wood, and estimates put the last round of coppicing here in the mid-1940s. The local council takes Kilminorth's management very seriously and currently has an ongoing thinning and coppicing regime, creating open glades for wildlife habitat and maintaining widespread access for visitors. Many paths traverse the wood and a bridleway also makes it suitable for horse riders and cyclists.

An ancient earth bank known as the Giant's Hedge follows the contours in the top of the wood. Hedges in Cornwall are, to all intents and purposes, earth banks which are usually built around large boulders, often being faced off with stones. In Kilminorth this 'hedge' is slightly underwhelming in stature, appearing mainly as a mossy bank, overgrown with old trees, ferns and brambles, with a track running alongside. Little hard fact is known about this extensive linear ancient monument, which may be traced some 15 miles westwards to the village of Lerryn, on the Fowey Estuary. It is generally thought to be post-Roman and possibly the boundary of some ancient Cornish kingdom. Apparently, the best-preserved part is in Willake Wood, near Lerryn, where it is up to 15 feet high in places. A charming little rhyming couplet about the hedge has endured for many years:

One day the Devil having nothing to do,
Built a great hedge from Lerryn to Looe.

SEA WOOD

Where trees almost tumble into Morecambe Bay

It is always rather special to find a wood which is happy sitting right on the very edge of the British coastline. Somehow astounding to see that trees can survive in the teeth of salt-laden gales or with their roots or lower branches trailing in the brackish sea water. Sea Wood, on the Cumbrian coast, south of Bardsea on the north-west shore of Morecambe Bay, is one of these places.

Sea Wood is a rare example of woodland occurring on boulder clay overlying Carboniferous limestone, and is the largest wood of its type in south Cumbria. Walking along the seaward side, it is most dramatically viewed from the beach, where trees almost tumble off a low limestone cliff into the briny. In fact, when tides are high and at their most ferocious this must occasionally happen as the cliff is gradually eaten away. The limestone boulders and pavement intrusions on the beach have been scoured and moulded for centuries by wave action, creating intriguing sculptural forms, sensual ridges and hollows, startling in their dazzling whiteness. Along the beach the bleached, bare-bone remains of tree stumps and boughs, some dumped from the wood above, others washed in from who-knows-where, litter the tide line, creating another open-air gallery of elemental sculptures. The tides run in very swiftly across the salt flats here and only a select few know the safe routes across Morecambe Bay's treacherous sands, so be extremely careful if you stray far from the shore. Bird lovers will get hours of pleasure watching the seabirds and waders feeding in the rich shallows.

The wood itself comprises 58 acres of ancient woodland with oak (mainly sessile), ash, sycamore and birch as the principal species, plus occasional wild cherry, some of which are large old pollards, wych elm, and an understorey of hazel, hawthorn and holly. Strangely, spindle and guelder rose are found only along the roadside margins. The presence of crab apple trees of some considerable age reaffirms the ancient pedigree of Sea Wood. The wonderfully pungent aroma of the vivid green crabs, nestling in circular carpets among the damp wood-floor detritus of autumn, is never forgotten. How mystifying that they smell so deceptively sweet. How disappointing that their sour bite ties your tongue in knots. If you like making jelly (a great accompaniment for game) or the splendid wine (one of my favourites) take a basket with you in October.

BELOW In the depths of the wood several old crab apple trees appear to have had an extremely productive year. These trees are perfect indicators of the wood's ancient origins.

RIGHT Sea Wood clings to the land above the low limestone cliff in Morecambe Bay. The boulder clay on top of the limestone is clearly visible here.

The wood has a long history and early records show that it once belonged to Lady Jane Grey until her sad and premature demise in the Tower in 1554. It was subsequently seized by the Crown, and that's the way matters remained until Lancashire County Council purchased it in the 1950s. Finally, in 1994, it was bought by the Woodland Trust. The peninsula on which Sea Wood is situated appears to be part of Cumbria, but was historically part of Lancashire (although currently administered by Cumbria). There is (apparently) plenty of evidence associated with the local copper-mining activities, with three old mine shafts and an adit to be found in the wood. (I looked, but could not pick out the mines from the jumble of hollows and boulders across the woodland floor.) Undoubtedly charcoal from coppice wood was used to fire the ore smelters. Records also show that oak timber was cut from the wood and floated at high tide along the coast to the shipyards at Ulverston. There are even stories of 'timber pirates' making off with the logs before they arrived at the shipyards.

Given the density of Sea Wood's vegetation, it is almost impossible to appreciate any of the great views out across Morecambe Bay. However, adjacent to the wood lies Birkrigg Common: a super open space of bracken, short sheep-cropped turf, the odd wind-bent hawthorn and a Neolithic stone circle – one of only thirty such double concentric circles in the UK (Stonehenge being the best-known example). The central, and most distinct, circle is 30 feet wide and made up of ten stones, the highest only standing about 3 feet tall, while the outer circle is 85 feet wide and has fifteen stones (mainly amid the bracken). The stones are of the local Carboniferous limestone, and the circle has been dated to the period 1700–1400BC. The site has long been known as the Druid's Temple. On a sunny day, with a stiff breeze buffeting you on this gentle hill, and the vast expansive panorama stretching over nearby Bardsea village, across the southern extremities of the Lake District, the yawn of Morecambe Bay to the edge of Sea Wood hard by, the whole place feels uplifting, invigorating and certainly not dark or mystical.

BELOW A typical autumn view through the oaks, ashes and sycamores inside the wood. With no sign of any sea here you might think yourself far inland.

RIGHT Birkrigg stone circle, above Sea Wood, and the view out over the village of Bardsea and Morecambe Bay.

OUT OF THE SWAMP

TATTERSHALL CARRS

Mighty alders on the fenland borders of Lincolnshire

If the natural interest within these two woods – Tattershall Carr and Tattershall Thorpe Carr – is more than slightly eclipsed by recent history and a human invasion of the habitat, it is perfectly understandable. Nature, as it so effectively does, is still slowly healing the remains of a mass occupation some 65 years ago.

Lying to the west of the small village of Tattershall Thorpe in Lincolnshire, these woods have a long, if ill-defined, history stretching back before 1600, placing them firmly in the category of ancient woodland. However, their character must have changed considerably over the last century. The name *carr* means wet woodland, though these are not the wettest of woods you will ever visit. In the past the water levels were much higher than they are today, but increasing agricultural demands for arable crops on the surrounding land brought improved drainage systems and this, together with gravel extraction which created man-made pits where water could collect, meant that water levels fell away and the once-dominant alder (always happiest with its feet in water) no longer held sway with the attendant grey willow. Birch, the great colonizer, made ground, and soon ash, oak and plenty of sycamore followed suit.

A walk today through Tattershall Carrs, celebrated as Lincolnshire's most extensive ancient alder carr woodland on fen-edge sands and gravels, reveals not just alder but also a diverse gathering of many broadleaved species. The birches have grown old enough to put on that silvery white bark riven by coarse splits, ridges and eruptions, advertising their aspirations of veteran status, so often elusive. Lofty ash and oak would appear to have been encouraged for some commercial intentions by long-departed foresters, and a handful of conifers and rhododendron suggest nineteenth-century attempts at softwood forestry or even some landscape design.

The understorey boasts rowan, holly, field maple and hazel. However, by far the most impressive trees here are the massive alder coppice stools, rising candelabra-like from the swathes of bracken or crouching expectantly above the wood-edge ditches, waiting for the swamp conditions that seldom prevail today, unless there have been prolonged spells of wet weather. Historic estate records show that these trees were regularly coppiced until the Second World War; for what purpose is uncertain, since alder wood doesn't make good firewood.

The year 1940 was a landmark for Tattershall Carrs. Britain was at war and the flat lands of Lincolnshire were ideal for airfields. RAF Coningsby was just to the south and RAF Woodhall Spa, a short step to the north, was opened in 1942. The woods provided perfectly natural, camouflaged cover for the many servicemen posted here. Construction work began in 1940, and over the next two years some hundred buildings were erected to provide accommodation and air-raid shelters for more than 1,000 men who were billeted in the woods. Perhaps the most famous group of airmen flying from Woodhall Spa during 1944 were 617 Squadron, 'the Dambusters', remembered for their notorious raids on the strategic dams of the Rühr Valley with their Lancaster bombers and the innovative bouncing bombs. Very occasionally visitors enjoying the tranquillity of Tattershall Carrs today may be transported back to those grim years as Britain's last remaining airworthy Lancaster bomber, part of the Battle of Britain Memorial Flight, roars into the air from nearby Coningsby, en route to some air pageant or display.

After the war was over most of the buildings in the woods were abandoned and slowly but surely they fell into dereliction. It's a strange and moving experience to discover the remains of these structures half hidden in the undergrowth

One of the wetter corners of Tattershall Carrs gives an indication of what much of the wood must have looked like before drainage ditches were dug around the perimeter.

today – memorials to a sense of duty, a fight for freedom and unconditional bravery. The scars of this relatively brief, but necessary, interlude in the history of Tattershall Carrs will take a long time to disappear completely, but even intensive habitation could not expunge centuries of ancient vegetation. In spring the woodland floor still bursts forth with snowdrops, followed by wood anemones, primroses, celandines, wood-sorrel, creeping jenny and, of course, bluebells. The damp ditches bear clumps of alternate-leaved and opposite-leaved golden saxifrages. The delicate, filigree fronds of climbing corydalis entwines rotting stumps and wood-floor

dead wood. A remarkable tally of 170 different plants have been recorded here. The sweet melodies of song thrushes lift the spirits, and in summer the gentle purring of turtle doves soothe. Woodcock, green and great spotted woodpeckers all call this home and garden warblers are summer visitors. There are bats here too – both British pipistrelle species as well as natterer's. The Woodland Trust has recently converted six of the derelict buildings into bat hibernacula (what a lovely word and one I've never had cause to write before!), and was rewarded last year when long-eared bats took up residence. There are also many summer-roosting

Massive old alder coppice stools, long outgrown and uncut, squat among the bracken.

bat boxes throughout the woods, offering year-round protection.

Ancient history, far below the sod where the Lancaster bombers rumbled by, has lately been revealed by the extraction of sand and gravel. Thousands of years ago, when this part of Britain was near the southern extremities of the ice sheet, fossil remains have shown that mammoth, woolly rhinoceros, bison and reindeer all roamed the prehistoric landscape.

ABOVE Just one of the numerous buildings and shelters within Tattershall Carrs which hark back to the dark days of the Second World War. Walking through the wood without meeting a soul it seems strange to think that hundreds of people were living here only 65 years ago. Nature is slowly erasing much of the evidence.

RIGHT Climbing corydalis envelopes a strange log 'beast' on the woodland floor.

COED Y CERRIG

Alder carr woods in a remote Gwent valley

Considering that this splendid wet woodland is bisected by a country lane, Coed y Cerrig still represents an impressive tract of alder carr across the valley bottom, and once in among the great old alders the road quickly blends into the background. Alder carr is a nationally endangered habitat type, now most often found in woods where management has simply been abandoned along with the drainage to provide drier conditions for more important timber trees.

In the past alder was one of the most sought-after trees to make the best charcoal, used particularly in the manufacture of gunpowder. Strong, yet light in weight, another widespread use for the wood was for clog pattens. Clogs were commonly worn by millworkers, miners and farm labourers in the north of England and in the industrialized South Wales valleys up to the middle of the twentieth century, but demand has all but disappeared, apart from a few specialist markets such as clogs for dancing.

Cwm Coed y cerrig is a narrow valley at the southern end of the Vale of Ewyas and although today it is a peaceful byway there is a sense that local industry was once supported by these woods. The nearby village of Forest Coal Pit, in the shadow of Sugar Loaf, must once have needed a multitude of pit props, and evidence of charred hearths dotted along the hillsides recalls charcoal production for the iron furnaces of south Wales.

BELOW The still waters of alder carr woodland make wonderful habitat for frogs and newts. In springtime the amorous males can make life difficult for the poor female frogs.

OPPOSITE Spring in the alder carr of Coed y Cerrig with wonderful swampy conditions which favour plants such as marsh marigolds.

LEFT Although quite small, this scarlet elf cap is a startling, bright red fungus of damp places.

RIGHT A slightly sinister little plant the toothwort grows off the roots of trees and has no chlorophyll.

BELOW There's a deeply primeval feel to these alder carr woods in the swampy valley bottom of Coed y Cerrig.

Opposite-leaved golden-saxifrage carpets many of the wetter flushes around the edge of the alder carr.

It is many a long year since any purposeful coppicing was undertaken in these woods, but the largest of the towering alders, which appear poised on their own individual islands amid the sopping, marshy woodland floor, are simply overgrown coppice stools. They have been left undisturbed for so long that they are now home to marvellous colonies of mosses and lichens. Where the water stands in pools or trickles idly by in aimless streams, the early spring brings golden splashes of marsh marigolds. On the wet margins fungi such as the vivid red scoops of scarlet elf cap (*Sarcoscypha coccinea*) jump out from last year's leaf litter. Often, in the damp flushes running down from the woods, the ground is covered in a greenish yellow mantle of opposite-leaved golden saxifrage. It is so tiny that you want a magnifying glass tucked in your pocket to fully appreciate its delicate beauty.

Access to the alder carr might be all but impossible if it wasn't for an excellent walkway built by the good folks of the Countryside Council for Wales. This circular boardwalk sits atop a pontoon of recycled motor-car tyres — surely a brilliant idea for using one of our most problematic waste products. Poke a stick into the oozing bog on either side and you'll soon realize that it could be disastrous to step off this thoughtfully provided route.

These wetlands are flanked along the protective, neighbouring hillsides by steeply graded woods of oak, ash, wych elm and hazel; while wrought and twisted beeches define the hilltops, before the wild moorland where windswept thorns break the barren skyline. On top of the hill to the north lies the Iron Age hillfort of Twyn y Gaer, worth the trek for the stupendous views in every direction. The woods are clearly ancient and there is much evidence of coppicing throughout. The bluebells are a treat in spring and there are also strange little flowers such as the rather insipid, slightly spooky-looking toothwort. A plant with no chlorophyll, it is a parasite which grows off the roots of trees, especially hazel, elm, alder and willow, and is so named for its tiers of slightly pinkish flowers which do have a passing resemblance to somewhat grubby, stained teeth or, as Peter Marren describes them, 'a set of dentures for a horse'. Here it appears to be growing mainly from the roots of old coppiced wych elms. Dutch elm disease certainly doesn't appear to have bothered these fine old trees as they throw out a healthy head of foliage each spring.

Various ancient tracks pass through these woods, many still roughly paved with stone or with banks shored up with slabs. There is a slightly lost, deserted feeling to this valley, compounded by the remains of several old settlements, long abandoned and crumbling away quietly amid the trees. It feels as if a once flourishing community has dwindled away to almost nothing. And still sheep bleat on the hill, birds sing in the woods, the river will flow for ever.

AROUND POND AND LAKE

DIMMINGS DALE

Erstwhile pleasure grounds of the gentry in a Staffordshire valley

The gateway to Dimmings Dale offers little obvious insight into its true natural splendour, its busy industrial past or its adoption as a rich man's showpiece wilderness. Only the unusual towered building, once a gatehouse on the Alton Towers Estate, but now flourishing as the Ramblers' Retreat, enticing weary walkers in for delicious refreshments, is a permanent reminder of its role as a garden extension. Two diverging forestry tracks lead you either side of the dammed River Churnet; now an impressive ornamental lake, but once the millpond for a thriving lead and iron-ore smelting works. Some of the buildings from the old works immediately below the lake still survive, but are now private dwellings.

The year 1800 was a pivotal time for Dimmings Dale. Around 150 years of industry drew to a close as the smelting of ore ceased, but the 15th Earl of Shrewsbury, Charles Talbot, was making huge improvements to Alton Towers and his outlying estate lands. Dimmings Dale's natural attributes must have fitted perfectly with the period's desire for tamed wilderness, although it seems likely that the Earl's love of tree planting extended to enhancing the valley, as some of the oldest beeches could well date back to the early nineteenth century. The broader tracks through the forest were once maintained as carriage rides for the pleasure of the Earls of Shrewsbury and their guests, who would drive down from the big house to sample a little of this rural idyll.

Walking into the valley, the sides become steeper above you. Here and there you catch a glimpse of dark sandstone crags looming beyond great oaks and dense vegetation. When the broadleaf cover breaks there are ranks of poker-straight Scots pines sweeping away to the distant upper edge of the valley. Modern forestry is

With the sunlight filtering through the woodland on a late summer's day it's obvious to see why the Victorians would have taken delight in their carriage rides through Dimmings Dale.

One of the splendid beeches along the carriage ride constructed for Charles Talbot, the 15th Earl of Shrewsbury, in the mid nineteenth-century. The tree was probably planted at the same time.

very much a part of this 643-acre site, yet most of the time a tranquil mood prevails.

To amble along the river bank is a delight at any time of year. The river is divided up into a series of serene ponds which, with the splash of their weirs and the babble of the intermittent rapids, creates a kind of 'quick-quick-slow' rhythm to the walk. With luck it's possible to catch sight of a kingfisher or perhaps a hungry heron waiting for a bite. There's usually a handful of mallard cruising the ponds and the distinctive staccato chatter of moorhens and coots. Although the large, lower pond clearly provided water power to drive hammers and bellows in the smelting works, the numerous other ponds would seem to bear no obvious purpose other than ornament, but maybe they were constructed as fish ponds – trout and crayfish still being abundant in the river.

The industrial history of this wood is still evident if you know how to look. Large coppice stools – particularly ash, oak and beech – are plentiful and, even though

coppicing was still active in the 1950s, many of these stools have not been cut since well before that time. Charcoal burning would have been the main reason for coppicing to provide fuel for the smelting works down the valley. Above the eastern bank of the river an old track with a beautiful mossy-bouldered, buttressing wall must have been the main thoroughfare through the valley, long before the broad carriage rides cut by the 15th Earl. Here and there little stone posts appear to mark boundaries or mileposts and there are signs of alder and beech which were once laid into hedges.

Even though the Forestry Commission has planted many a pine on the valley sides, it has also planted broadleaved species such as oak, beech and sweet chestnut. However, in the valley bottom the natural vegetation still holds sway. Large oaks and beeches are plentiful and some impressive alders bestride the boggy margins of the river. There's a smattering of wild cherry, birch and small-leaved lime, with hazel and holly throughout the understorey. In springtime

ABOVE Sun struggles through the early morning mist across the lake at Alton Towers, a scene far more fitting the gentility of nineteenth-century garden promenades rather than the high-energy entertainment park of today.

RIGHT Autumn leaves caught on the lip of one of the weirs below a pond show that oak, beech, birch and sycamore are the principal broadleaf trees of the Dale.

bluebells, wood anemones and wood-sorrel bedeck the woodland floor. In autumn the mellow gold of the beech foliage casts sumptuous reflections in the pools. Another season's lost leaves glide across the mirrored surface, before slipping gently out of the calm into the rough and tumble of the river ride or, if they are lucky, catching on the rim of the weir, poised above the void. Will they, or won't they, plummet?

There is something strangely synonymous between these leaves on their final journey and the rollicking, gut-wrenching rides at nearby Alton Towers theme park, barely a mile or two over the hill. Who can forget the tension in the gentle ascent of the hairiest of rides? That unstoppable muscle tightening; the nervous whispers and giggles; the sudden desire to step off; that fleeting moment of hanging on the brink and the inevitable death-defying hurtle to oblivion … or perhaps safe harbour at the end of the ride, like some lost leaf finding landfall.

STOURHEAD

A sylvan lakeside setting in Wiltshire; one of England's greatest gardens

Popularly regarded as one of the finest eighteenth-century gardens in Britain, Stourhead, in Wiltshire, is truly one of the most remarkable, romantic landscapes incorporating trees and still water you could ever wish to find. The house and gardens were given by Sir Henry Hoare to the National Trust in 1946, which now has the challenge of maintaining the original landscape integrity of these classic gardens with an eye on conservation issues and the practicalities of accommodating some 350,000 visitors every year.

It is difficult to imagine what the garden must first have looked like in the mid-eighteenth century, with its newly created lake and a host of planted trees and shrubs, albeit with a natural backdrop of the existing woodland, although late-eighteenth-century prints give an inkling. The whole scheme was the brainchild of Henry Hoare II who, upon inheriting the Stourhead Estate in 1741, began to transform the gentle valley of the River Stour, near to his great Palladian mansion, into a wonderful garden. Hoare's vision for his garden was largely influenced by painters such as Claude Lorrain and Gaspard Dughet and their Utopian, stylized Italian landscapes, frequently adorned with all manner of classical temples and gazebos. For the gardeners of the eighteenth century it signalled a break with the rigidity of French-influenced designs, full of geometric patterns and formal borders. Strangely enough, though, the new vogue for these Arcadian landscapes was simply adopting a different formality; and yet, as it broke with existing tastes, it must have felt liberating and radical at the time.

While Hoare oversaw the damming of the river to create the lake and began his tree planting, he commissioned the architect Henry Flitcroft to design and build a series of classically inspired follies around the lake. The Temple of Flora was the first to be completed in 1746, followed by the Pantheon, the Temple of Apollo, the quaint little Gothic Cottage and, beneath a rocky mound on the lake's edge, the Grotto. In the depths of the Grotto a reclining figure of Ariadne slumbers peacefully on her marble plinth, while the cleverly rerouted waters of the Stour trickle past her for eternity. Delicate geometric patterns of tiny pebbles in the floor contrast with the coarse volcanic rock, brought all the way from Italy, which lines the walls. Here all is cool, calm, if a little dank; a simple, contemplative place; a retreat from all that arboreal grandeur outside. Cut in the marble slabs before Ariadne is a short poem by the fifteenth-century Cardinal Bembo, translated by Alexander Pope:

Nymph of the grot these sacred springs I keep
And to the murmur of these waters sleep
Ah spare my slumbers gently tread the cave
And drink in silence or in silence lave.

Sweeping and serpentine paths and drives laid the garden open for the pleasure and entertainment of the family's guests, the various features providing focal points along the tour, where tea could be taken or views admired. When the renowned landscaper Humphry Repton remarked that 'the beauty of a lake consists not so much in its size, as in those deep bays and bold promontories which prevent the eye from ranging over its whole surface', he might well have had Stourhead in mind.

From 1791 Henry's son, Richard Colt Hoare, began planting in earnest. In tune with much of the surrounding woodland, a lot of beech was planted, as well as oak, but the garden gradually became a wonderful collection of conifers from all over the world. The first half of the nineteenth century was a period of exotic-tree introduction like no

View across the lake at Stourhead towards the Pantheon, beyond the rich, golden yellow of a fine tulip tree on the island.

A View from the Pantheon, in Mr Hoare's Garden at Stourton, in Wiltshire.

LEFT This copper engraving dating from around 1770 shows 'A View from the Pantheon in Mr. Hoare's Garden at Stourton in Wiltshire'. The Mount of Diana, beyond the islands to the left, does not appear to exist any more, or at least is now shrouded in trees.

BELOW View across the lake to the Palladian bridge.

other, and many landowners developed a highly competitive spirit and a strong desire to show off to their peers. To have the rarest species or acquire brand-new introductions before any of your immediate neighbours or gardening chums became a consuming passion. The result – a marvellous array of specimen trees from North America, Japan, Eurasia and China hold the stage at Stourhead.

A walk around the margin of the lake offers

Ariadne slumbers in her Grotto behind the lake's edge at Stourhead. The figure is cast in lead, painted white, and was created by John Cheere for Henry Flitcroft, who built the grotto in 1748.

ever-changing views with endless variations in the balance and range of tree shapes and sizes as well as contrasting or complementary tones and colours which the seasons ordain. There are a few record-breaking trees here – some of the rare pines and spruces being the tallest examples in Britain. A phenomenal western red cedar with its multiple stems – some probably layerings, others root suckers – is a great tree cavern in itself. Splendid, solitary trees stand in glorious isolation, and perhaps few more arresting than a couple of fine tulip trees: one on the little island in the middle of the lake, and another on the south side of the lake, which must be one of the greatest-girthed specimens in Britain. The latter tree quite possibly dates back to the early years of planting, putting it in excess of 200 years old. The deep buttery yellow of tulip trees in autumn is spectacular. The glorious reds, oranges and yellows of the Japanese maples complete the autumn colour-fest. In spring it's down to the banks of rhododendrons and azaleas to draw the eye.

If anything, some of the views are now starting to appear a little crowded. So often, the previous generations of planters got a little carried away with squeezing in more and more trees which, when they were relatively small, wasn't a problem. In maturity there's a risk that some trees begin to lose their form and may well overwhelm smaller specimens or interest in the shrub layer.

Across the slopes above the eastern side of the lake, an area known as the Shades, a bit of woodland management is currently under way to re-establish the original vision of high trees, mainly beech, casting dappled shade across ground cover of cherry laurel. An interesting insight into J.C. Loudon's view of this scheme emerges from his *Arboretum et Fruticetum* in 1838. 'In the woods at Stourhead, the laurel undergrowths are unmixed with any other tree or shrub, except large beech trees; and the effect of a mass of shining evergreens beneath these lofty beeches, though powerful, is yet extremely monotonous.' Even though the National Trust, in deference to the original landscape plan, is resurrecting this feature, I must confess to concurring with Mr Loudon's opinion.

FROM FOUR CORNERS OF THE WORLD

KEW GARDENS

At the heart of botanical excellence in Britain

A fascinating little book entitled *Beauties and Wonders of Vegetable Life* was published by the Religious Tract Society in the 1860s and perfectly encapsulated Kew's transformation from private garden to public park:

In the year 1840 [1841 seems a more accurate date] the grounds around the old Kew Palace, instead of being a private royal garden, were thrown open to the public. Before that time there might be seen one or two carriages standing at the gate, while a party of gentlefolks entered the gardens. Then the working man and his family, if spending a day's holiday in the country, could only peep over the hedge or wall; but now the humblest are at liberty to enjoy the beauties of the place as well as their richer neighbours, and behold some of the wonders of creation, which, when rightly understood, may make them wiser and happier than they were before.

The story of Kew is a long and convoluted tale, which could easily fill a book this size and more. The evolution of the gardens emanates from the early years of the eighteenth century, when the adjacent estates of Richmond and Kew were acquired by the royal family. Frederick, Prince of Wales and his wife Princess Augusta settled at Kew in 1731, slowly transforming their 100-acre garden with the assistance of their friend Lord Bute, an inspired and passionate horticulturalist. However, the true beginnings of Kew as it is known today date from 1759, when Princess Augusta began in earnest to create a physic garden that she fully intended would, in the words of Lord Bute, 'contain all the plants known on Earth'.

The greatest strides forward in the development of Kew in those early years were largely down to one man – Sir Joseph Banks – an intrepid voyager, explorer and botanist, who had sailed with Captain Cook. From 1773 he became a close friend and adviser to George III and was given responsibility for expanding the gardens. In that year alone he oversaw the planting of almost 800 different tree species at Kew. The plant collection grew and the new drive actively to send collectors all over the world was fired by Banks, who could see the commercial potential in building global links for the interchange of plants and information. 'He visualized Kew as a storehouse of knowledge and research which could be used to good advantage. It was on his vision of the future that Kew grew and developed,' writes Madeleine Bingham in *The Making of Kew*.

With the death in 1820 of both George III and Banks, interest and royal patronage of Kew slumped, and the gardens weathered a period of general decline, only to be revived in 1841 when the Treasury deemed them worthy of saving and transferred them from the Crown to the Department of Woods and Forests. Sir William Hooker was appointed director and from that point on Kew never looked back. The 1840s were a remarkable period. Acquisition of more of the surrounding estate boosted the gardens to 250 acres. William Andrews Nesfield was commissioned to redesign the arboretum – a scheme that is still largely evident today – and the Palm House, perhaps Kew's most definitive building, was completed to great acclaim in 1848.

Today the Palm House still feels as though it is very much the centrepiece; instantly recognizable, this 360-foot-long behemoth of a glasshouse with its 45,000 square feet of glass was designed by Decimus Burton and took four years to build. The vast scale of the building makes it a great landmark by which to maintain your bearings as you navigate the gardens.

A stunning tree for autumn colour is this American smoke tree (*Cotinus obovartus*).

It doesn't matter what time of year you go to Kew, there's always something to see. The autumn colours are a real treat, with the towering golden columns of the tulip trees or the myriad golds and reds of the Japanese maples. Children (and quite a few adults) will love collecting the greatest variety of leaves you could find anywhere. As autumn fades, just enjoy kicking through the leaves, inhaling that strangely reassuring damp, leafy smell. Winter, in the snow, brings that muffled hush to the gardens that only snow can; the seemingly limitless collection of conifers from every corner of the world hung heavy, until it all becomes too much and a mini-avalanche cascades down, landing with a soft whump. The remarkable bare-branch geometry of the broadleaved trees, stark against a leaden sky, awaiting the next fall. In spring, the vibrant greens of young leaves bursting from the bud, the blowsy white or pink flowers of the magnolia collection – perfect for a moment, but rusty-rimmed from the slightest frost. Then, as spring drifts towards summer, the famous Rhododendron Dell is at its very best. High summer on the edge of the city can be hot … and it may be getting hotter, so what could be better than escaping to the welcome shade of the huge old specimen trees with their broad canopies? Massive planes, towering chestnut-leaved oaks or veteran sweet chestnuts, some of which may date back to the late seventeenth century.

If you want to escape the hurly-burly on a fine weekend, make for the south-west corner of the gardens and discover the 40 acres of the Natural Area around Queen Charlotte's Cottage. Gifted by Queen Victoria in 1898, her only stipulation was that this part of Kew Gardens should remain wild; and so it is to this day. Carpets of bluebells wander where they will, more than twenty badger setts lie hidden in the undergrowth, dead-wood habitat is littered about to encourage wildlife and if you're lucky you might spot the rare white-letter hairstreak butterfly on the wing. Watch out too for the 'loggery' with its giant carved stag beetles clambering over it. It is hoped that this specially created habitat will attract these rare insects.

Drifting back towards the gates, you may think that the aliens have landed or some mammoth fairground attraction has moved in. In fact it's one of Kew's latest additions, the Treetop Walkway. Built on massive steel pillars, it carries you 59 feet aloft to walk among the branches of some of the gardens' splendid broadleaved trees. Tony Kirkham – Kew's top tree man and familiar to many from the BBC programmes – is very proud

of his 'new baby', although he concedes that some critics weren't over-impressed with this transgression on part of the Capability Brown landscape. Mr Brown was at the cutting edge of his profession in the eighteenth century, so there's every chance that he'd have been pretty enthusiastic about a feature like this today. Idly daydreaming, gazing out across the gardens, you might be startled by a raucous screech at close quarters. Bizarrely, it's a large emerald-green Ring-necked Parakeet. One of Britain's latest arrivals, and hugely successful ones at that, somehow Kew feels like the most appropriate place for them to be.

One of the most famous trees at Kew Gardens is the Old Lion Ginkgo – one of the original trees which dates back to the early years of Kew, being planted there by Lord Bute in 1762. The tree had been grown from the first seeds brought to Britain from China in 1754.

RIGHT This beautiful spreading Indian horse chestnut (var. Sidney Pearce) is one of several such trees at Kew. A splendid-looking tree, offering good late flowering (this is June - so about a month after our naturalized horse chestnut has flowered) and useful shade, it should be planted more often in Britain.

BELOW LEFT One of the latest attractions for visitors, the amazing new Treetop Walkway towers 59 feet overhead.

BELOW RIGHT Some of the remarkable magnolias at Kew provide a superb display in early spring.

WESTONBIRT

The National Arboretum in Gloucestershire, grown glorious from a nineteenth-century vision

There are many tree collections to be found the length and breadth of Britain and almost without exception they are the fruits of diligent labours, extremely deep pockets and arboreal passions of wealthy nineteenth-century gentry and landowners. The collecting of plants and trees reached its apotheosis during the mid-nineteenth century. Landowners with large estates had seen the fashions and fads of the landscape movement come and go. They had vied with each other for the services of the foremost landscape designers – Brown, Kent, Bridgeman, Repton et al. They craved the most expansive views, the largest serpentine lakes, the most artistic clumps of ancient trees, the most romantic follies and eyecatchers, all to be shown off to their guests (and most especially their neighbours) as they approached their great houses along the longest of meandering drives.

Early introductions of exotic trees had begun in the seventeenth century. The Tradescants were famous for their garden at Lambeth and Henry Compton, Bishop of London, boasted some splendid specimen trees in his garden at Fulham Palace, his emissary John Bannister bringing new trees from America. During the eighteenth century the plant hunters had begun to return with ever more specimens, and by the early nineteenth century virtually every corner of the globe had given up at least some of its arboreal treasures. International communications had improved – botanical collections around the world were exchanging specimens and knowledge.

So when, in 1829, the young Robert Stayner Holford began planting trees on the family estate at Westonbirt, in Gloucestershire, he was undoubtedly doing the same as many of his friends, acquaintances and 'gardening rivals' near and far. It seems a strange coincidence that he chose 1829 to start his planting, for it's possible that he may have been influenced by the return of David Douglas

BELOW This photograph from around 1910 shows two fine English elms at Westonbirt. These are undoubtedly in the grounds surrounding the old house (now a private school) across the road from the arboretum. What makes the picture particularly interesting is that the elderly gentleman in the carriage is almost certainly George Holford, son of Robert.

RIGHT View along Mitchell Drive in the spring with a sunrise horse chestnut in the foreground.

ENGLISH ELMS
Near Down Gate

With an avowed intent to build one of the very best collections of maples at Westonbirt, this paperbark maple shows the rich variety of colour in just one tree.

from his second plant-hunting expedition to America in 1827. He had brought 210 new species back, including Douglas fir and western yellow pine. Over the following thirty years an avalanche of important, beautiful and useful conifers would arrive in Britain – the deodar, noble fir, grand fir, Sitka spruce, Monterey pine, Atlas cedar, coast redwood and, of course, the forest giant, the Sierra or giant redwood – to the chagrin of the Americans, our Wellingtonia and not Washingtonia.

The land Holford chose for his pleasure grounds was rich, fertile, and well supplied with underground springs. His first task was to plant shelter belts of oak, laurel, pine and yew to protect some of the more tender specimens. Then began the joyous task of designing and planting avenues and rides that radiated out from his house. There were also extensive grounds around the family home, richly adorned with trees. In the 1920s this became a private school, but still has many of its original plantings.

There was pride to be taken in planting newly introduced species or a brand-new cultivar before anyone else. Robert Holford had a competitive spirit, frequently entertaining or visiting his arch-rival Lord Ducie, who owned a neighbouring estate

to the west, so that they could show off their latest acquisitions or propagating successes; what have amusingly been termed 'sneering parties'. However, regardless of this one senses that Holford was a true 'tree man' for he went at his planting with a passion for more than sixty years, also being joined by his son George in the 1870s. It was George who expanded the arboretum into the adjacent Silk Wood, carving rides through the ancient woodland and planting yet more exotic species. When George died in 1926 he and his father had managed to create one of the finest arboreta in Britain.

The Forestry Commission acquired Westonbirt in the late 1950s, via the Crown, in lieu of death duties, and has spent the last fifty years making it into the National Arboretum. The statistics are impressive. The site covers some 600 acres, with 17 miles of paths. There are 4,000 different species of trees and shrubs and 18,500 listed specimens; with 104 champion trees and 109 species that are endangered or extinct in the wild (figures which will undoubtedly be out of date as soon as this book is published).

Set aside the superlatives and simply get there and explore this unparalleled repository of the world's trees. The old arboretum still contains many of the

To the uninitiated these may look like a bunch of rather twiggy bushes. Far from it. These groups are the remaining stems of an ancient small-leaved lime coppice stool discovered a few years ago in Silk Wood. All from the same tree, it is thought to be well in excess of 2,000 years old.

original specimens which Robert Holford brought in from around the globe. Huge North American conifers in their full majesty are complemented by many special and unusual broadleaf specimens. A host of different magnolias add colour and lift the spirits in spring, while Japanese maples are ablaze with every shade of red and gold in the autumn. Saunter through the dappled shade of giant oriental planes and the impressive lime avenue. Better than a book; if you want to learn about trees this is surely the best place to come, for everything is systematically labelled … and pretty well every tree is here.

Exploring nearby Silk Wood is different from the old arboretum, for here the blend of exotic species is interwoven with the ancient oak woods. Cedars, monkey puzzles, redwoods, firs and pines grow about the rides, while the compartments contain comprehensive broadleaf collections – ash, oak, cherry and maple. Westonbirt is striving to have the biggest and best collection of Japanese maples in the world; already heading towards 300 species, that competitive spirit is still alive and well here. The native roots of Silk Wood haven't been forgotten, though, as compartments of natural oak and ash wood are still being actively coppiced with standards.

Until fairly recently a little-known jewel lay hidden in Silk Wood which, by great good fortune, George Holford had just happened to miss during his improvements. However, in the 1970s, during some proposed changes, several clumps of small-leaved lime were about to be dug up and removed when John White, then curator, realized that he might have found something unusual. He enlisted the help of Oliver Rackham and between them they decided to have a DNA analysis done across the group of coppice stools. The result confirmed that this was all one tree – the groups were actually the fragmented or dispersed stems from a single lime. Best estimate by Rackham was an age of at least 2,000 years, making this by far the oldest tree at Westonbirt.

Westonbirt is brilliantly set up for family visits, and can happily accommodate people of all abilities, with superb facilities and a regular annual round of special events, including courses, guided walks, exhibitions, talks, concerts and a recent popular attraction, running up to Christmas, when the arboretum is floodlit with coloured lights. The Forestry Commission is even happy to have dogs in Silk Wood – my Scotties Molly and Phoebe certainly gave it the paws-up.

BELOW Last of a December
day's sunshine reveals the
watchful spirit of the ancient
sweet chestnut.

OPPOSITE Late afternoon
sun glances across the front
of Croft Castle - more a
crenellated house than a
defensive stronghold.

GREAT HOUSES, GREAT PARKS

CROFT CASTLE ESTATE

A grand gathering of ancient trees populate this historic parkland in Herefordshire

About 6 miles north-west of the Herefordshire market town of Leominster lies Croft Castle and its wonderful estate which is so richly endowed with a mixture of woodland, ancient trees, avenues and all sorts of surprising and notable tree features. If you want a day to immerse yourself in all matters arboreal, Croft is the place to go. Naturally the castle itself is of great interest too, although it is not the most imposing of buildings. Of fourteenth-century origin, the structure you see today is largely a seventeenth-century castellated manor house with much eighteenth-century remodelling. Evidence of a medieval castle has been excavated immediately to the west of the present building.

The estate at Croft extends to around 1,500 acres, and an excellent network of footpaths opens up most of this for your enjoyment. Croft's woodlands, which sweep around the north side of the castle's surrounding parkland in a broad protective belt, comprise many different types of stands. There are areas of broadleaved woodland, many of which have been overplanted, and yet there is still evidence in the ground flora that these are ancient woods. There are also stands exclusively of beech, which show little evidence of historic woodland, although the dense shade of beech could well have overcome what ancient flora was once there.

Quite a lot of Croft's woodlands are under intensive conifer plantations, mainly on land that the Forestry Commission has leased since the 1930s. At that time, and in the immediate aftermath of the Second World War, there was a huge demand for timber. Government directives demanded massive increases in softwood production, and the outer limits of Croft's ancient parkland were right in the path of the tree planters. Scores of ancient oaks and sweet chestnuts were poisoned, ring-barked or pushed over to make way for pine, larch, spruce and western

hemlock. A walk in these woods today is an eerie step back into the past, for among the conifers the ghosts of mighty, ancient trees squat in the gloom; their dank boles jagged, broken and blackened in death. And yet they harbour life, for many are cloaked in mosses and lichens. Rare and specialized communities of invertebrates need this habitat. Bold birches or rowans swagger from the loamy interiors while upstart, cheeky, self-seeded hemlocks find purchase in any available nook or cranny.

We live in more enlightened times, thank goodness. It is inconceivable that such ancient parkland trees would be sacrificed in this fashion for modern forestry. In fairness to the Forestry Commission, its current policies for the conservation of ancient trees and broadleaved woodland are to be commended. At Croft it is working in concert with the National Trust to give the ancient trees which are still alive the best possible management and chance of a long-term future. With luck and a spirit of adventure you may find a small clearing in the conifers where a dozen or so massive old oak pollards stand among the swaying fronds of bracken. Hollow they may be; battered, bent or stag-headed, but they are still in good heart.

Heading for the highest ground, you should arrive at Croft Ambrey, an impressive Iron Age hill fort, its well-defined ramparts enclosing a 32-acre settlement which has been dated to 1050BC. Even allowing for the surrounding woods, which have partially obscured the 360-degree panorama, you can still appreciate its prominent, defensible significance, with far-reaching views west to Wales and north into Shropshire. Archaeological investigations in the 1960s concluded that the site was continuously occupied from the sixth century BC until AD48. The discovery of burnt buildings from this last date makes it seem likely that the settlement was overcome and destroyed by the Romans.

Below the outer edge of the western and northern ramparts of the hillfort is a very strange planting of dozens of hornbeams. Although a native species, hornbeam is a relatively uncommon tree in this part of the country, so one would expect it to have been planted for a specific purpose – its extremely hard wood often being used for the cogs of water mills. By strange coincidence an eighteenth-century water mill, in the care of English Heritage, sits by the River Lugg at nearby Mortimer's Cross. Judging by their size, these hornbeams must be around 200 years old, but making connections could be intriguing. On the other hand they may be purely ornamental.

Back into the parkland proper, closer to the castle, the most exciting trees are the monstrous, ancient sweet chestnuts. The remains of an avenue which runs from the north to the castle contains some of the most imposing individual trees, their great boles a mass of grotesque writhing forms. Sadly, however, many have been blighted by a water-borne disease called phytopthora which is slowly killing many trees and has seen off a few already. There is no cure for trees as ancient as these; the only hope is that some will survive the

Beech woods above Fishpool Valley in winter.

Winter etches the rugged lines of an ancient oak pollard in a small clearing between the massed ranks of conifers around the Croft Estate.

attack. Meanwhile, those that have died stand as towering natural sculptures, their bleached bare corkscrew limbs clawing at the heavens.

To the west of the castle another avenue of chestnuts leads away to an unknown destination or gateway. Those closest to the castle are the oldest and, like the trees to the north, may well have been planted 400 to 450 years ago. The more remote trees run for half a mile as a triple avenue – the only one like it in Britain. This feature has no obvious function as a thoroughfare, but recent opinion suggests that it could be a chestnut orchard. Remarkably, Croft never came under the radical remodelling influences of any of the great eighteenth-century landscapers. The competitive spirit of landscape enhancement bypassed Croft completely; particularly strange given that the estate was set firmly between those great movers and shakers of the Picturesque movement –

Uvedale Price at Foxley and Richard Payne Knight at Downton. The retention of so many great sweet chestnuts might well have reflected the deep affection held for the species by adherents to the Picturesque ethic.

There are no longer any deer in the deer park (apart from those that frequently sneak in from the adjoining woodland), but the abundance of ancient pollard sweet chestnuts and oaks confirm that a grazing regime among the old trees has prevailed here for centuries; witness the cattle and sheep still roaming the park today. A couple of gems to seek out are some gigantic small-leaved limes on the lawns to the south of the castle and, if you can find it in its secretive, shady defile, Britain's biggest sessile oak grows in the park, with a great burry bole some 37 feet around, a tree that could easily be 1,000 years old. Happy hunting.

BELOW Spring in Ickworth
Park among the ancient oaks.
An agricultural landscape
of fields and hedges
which became a park
300 years ago.

OPPOSITE The unique
appearance of Ickworth
House with its 100-foot-high
rotunda, amid the formal
gardens.

ICKWORTH ESTATE

Invitation to a tea party in an eighteenth–century Suffolk park

One of the jewels in the crown of Suffolk's treescapes is the stunning park and woodland of the Ickworth Estate, some 3 miles south-west of Bury St Edmunds. Undulating pastoral sweeps where the sheep peacefully graze among hoary old veteran oaks surround the unique architectural centrepiece. Ickworth is a remarkable neoclassical house built by the Hervey family between 1795 and 1821. Today its giant 100-foot-high rotunda and imposing 600-foot-long façade, as well as the impressive formal gardens, which include the Gold and Silver Gardens, the Temple Rose Garden and the bizarre Victorian Stumpery, command

the attention of the multitudes who visit. There are many fine ornamental and exotic trees in the immediate environs of the house, with the lawns dominated by a group of towering cedars, but it would be interesting to know how many visitors appreciate the wealth of native trees scattered throughout the 1,800 acres of glorious parkland.

The Hervey family lived here from 1467 until a few years ago although, in 1956, they were obliged to pass the house, park and a large endowment to the National Trust in lieu of death duties. The original family home was a manor house, built in the late fifteenth century, on lower ground to the

south-west of the present edifice; between the medieval church (now derelict) and the River Linnet. This area still bears the remnants of the 1st Earl of Bristol's eighteenth-century garden – a summerhouse, walled garden (now a vineyard) and canalized section of the river. An area a little to the west, still well endowed with old oak pollards, is known as the Old Deer Park, and it is supposed that this was the original thirteenth-century deer park; a licence for about 50 acres of imparking being granted between 1259 and 1264.

In 1655 the whole estate amounted to 1,188 acres, the majority of which comprised small fields with hedgerows, blocks of woodland, farmsteads and cottages. By the beginning of the eighteenth century the Herveys had swept away these farms and villages, rehousing the ousted tenants in nearby Horringer, expanding their park and reintroducing the deer. There are records of the 2nd Earl employing the great Capability Brown between 1769 and 1776 and, even though Brown's accounts fail to give details of exactly what work was done, scholars feel that many of the views and plantings bear out his influence. It is said that Charles Bridgeman and Thomas Wright were also consulted during the eighteenth century, yet no records of their actual involvement with the estate landscaping exist.

To those interested in landscape history a visit to Ickworth is at once a puzzling experience. First instincts indicate a medieval deer park with its wealth of old pollard trees liberally scattered throughout. Oliver Rackham has squashed this misconception by revealing the lost agricultural landscape, documented in detail in *The Ickworth Survey Boocke* of 1665, which was eradicated during the imparking of 1701. Cottages, farms and hedges may have disappeared, but the framework of trees that connected them all survives in some order to this day, creating what Rackham calls a 'pseudo-medieval park'.

Walk in the park and you can find linear alignments of old oak pollards – ancient hedges – and sometimes the banks on which they grew. Many of these trees are, as you would expect, well in excess of 300 years old. The woodland cover must have changed too; for at the northern end of the estate, in what is now pasture land along the river valley, there are some mighty field maple coppice stools. One in particular, with an astounding girth of 24 feet, must have been released from its woodland captivity at least 200 or 300 years ago otherwise it would not have survived

LEFT Discovered in open pasture near the River Linnet, this humungous field maple coppice stool has an astounding girth of 24 feet, making it one of the biggest and oldest of its kind in Britain. Best estimates for age are about 500 years old.

OPPOSITE Probably the oldest oak in Ickworth Park is The Tea Party Oak, so named because the local children from nearby Horringer would come and take tea beneath its vast spreading boughs. That was obviously quite a while ago. It is thought to be 700-800 years old.

the browsing beasts of the park. How old might this maple actually be? Also, in what appears to be an abandoned quarry set above the valley, evidence of extremely old bricks tipped into a hole gave pause for thought. Could these be part of one of the cottages or hamlets demolished at the park expansion of 1701? Walking the estate with your eyes peeled takes you on a trail of detection and discovery.

Occasionally you will encounter some truly amazing individual trees at Ickworth. Right by the car park are a pair of wonderful oak pollards, bent and hollow, but still hale and hearty; they have been locked in an arboric dialogue for at least a couple of centuries. Across the old greensward the Methuselah of the park – the squat giant frame of the Tea Party Oak, estimated to be about 700 to 800 years old – beckons you over with its bleached, claw-like lateral bough. So called because the village children of nearby Horringer used to take tea beneath its great spreading canopy, its verdant head is now considerably more modest. The old tree has pulled in its horns, retrenching for as long a senescence as possible. Back down the park to the river valley, where the quarry lies on the hill, and here an improbable oak seems to squat on its extensive root system like some giant crab. Perched only on a small mound of flint-pocked clay the old tree appears poised for action. Its longest root (above ground) stretches 33 feet from the bole. Jon Stokes, from the Tree Council, and I have informally named this tree the Flint Oak.

MARKS OF MANKIND

HACKFALL

A Georgian woodland wilderness garden amid the Yorkshire Dales

It might not appear immediately obvious to the casual observer, but Hackfall is actually a Grade 1 listed garden, although beneath this picturesque setting lies one of Yorkshire's finest ancient woods. The densely wooded gorge of Hackfall rises some 350 feet above a great bend in the River Ure to the pretty village of Grewelthorpe; and the woodland has been subjected to a long history of embellishment and management, of which a whole new cycle is just beginning.

Hackfall is in the ownership of the Woodland Trust and is leased to and managed by the Hackfall Trust, a group of locally based folk who have long held affections and concerns for the site. Recent events have shown how the plans for this remarkable ancient wood could so easily have taken a turn towards a theme park. Common sense prevailed and the formation of the Hackfall Trust in the 1980s set out to secure and conserve a unique wooded landscape park for future generations. Partnership with the Woodland Trust in 1987 led to a more detailed understanding of the ecological importance of Hackfall which, when viewed in association with its garden history and architectural features, makes it such a special place.

Records show that John Aislabie, responsible for the landscaping at nearby Studley Royal, purchased Hackfall in 1731 for the princely sum of £906. He had plans for transforming the wood for the delight and entertainment of his guests, but it was his son William who undertook the great transformation, turning Hackfall into a 'beautiful wilderness' between 1750 and 1767. An extensive network of paths was laced with surprise viewpoints, waterfalls, cascades, follies and grottoes. A lyrical appreciation of Hackfall appears in *The Penny Magazine* for 1835:

Without minutely detailing the successive cascades, and other objects and points of view which intervene, it may suffice to mention that an arrangement of the most interesting walks, through landscapes that cannot be excelled in variety and picturesque effect, lead to several romantic situations in pleasing succession, and at length to the summit of a rock called Mowbray Point, a commanding eminence, from which the most grand and extensive prospects are obtained. Mr Gilpin [Reverend William Gilpin, who coined the expression 'picturesque'] says that he scarcely remembers to have anywhere seen an extensive view so full of beauties and so free from faults.

HACKFALL.

[Alum Spring at Hackfall, Yorkshire.]

LEFT A wood engraving showing a view of the Alum Springs at Hackfall, as depicted in *The Penny Magazine* of 1835. These cascades still exist, but certainly look rather more impressive in this early print than they do in actuality.

OPPOSITE A photograph taken in the middle of Hackfall in 1995 shows how overgrown the whole place had become, the cascades beneath the vegetation barely visible. Sensitive felling and clearing some of the dense understorey in recent times has revealed the original 'garden' scheme.

Throughout the nineteenth century Hackfall became an important resort for tourists. Refreshments could be taken at Mowbray Point, one of the follies, where the Aislabies had once entertained their guests. Wordsworth commended Hackfall to his readers in a tourist guide of 1810. Turner visited in 1816 and was inspired to paint a view along the river from Sandbird Hut. Ramblers could discover Mowbray Castle, a sham medieval ruin; the Grotto with its attendant Cascade in view; the Rustic Temple with Fountain Pond; the octagonal Fisher's Hall, clad with limestone petrifications (still partly intact today) and, at many a turn, superb views through the wood or out across the surrounding countryside. The Victorians were captivated by Hackfall and accounts tell of 30,000 people visiting every year.

From around 1910 trees were felled on an irregular basis, but in 1934, when the wood had been sold to a timber merchant, huge quantities of mature timber were extracted. It is said that much damage was caused during this period, but Hackfall was then neglected for the next 50 years, so that by the time the Hackfall Trust was formed the landscape garden had degenerated into a tangled, impenetrable mess and most of the follies and grottoes were derelict. Today, with the benefit of some sensitive management and substantial Heritage Lottery funding to restore the original features of the eighteenth-century Aislabie scheme, Hackfall has had something of a renaissance, and a bright future is assured.

A visit today offers a brand-new parking place for your car a little to the north of Grewelthorpe village. Before you hurtle off into the wood, enjoy the massive old sycamore pollards set along the nearby drystone wall – two absolute beauties in their northern heartland. How thoughtful too that

After a little carefully considered tree felling the remarkable vista from Mowbray Point, out across the gorge, has recently been restored. You might enjoy this most special view while you take breakfast on the terrace, as the Landmark Trust have just restored the folly at Mowbray Point and made it available for holiday letting.

A flight of the original stone steps installed by William Aislabie at Hackfall in the mid eighteenth-century.

the Hackfall Trust has left maps of the wood (or perhaps, more properly, the 'park') at the gate for you to borrow on your walk. The top of the wood boasts some mighty beeches, particularly beautiful in spring or autumn, but this is essentially a wood of oak, birch, wych elm, sycamore, a surprising amount of small-leaved lime (not a common tree in northern climes), alder near the riverside, and an understorey of holly, rowan, hazel and the occasional spindle. A few of the great vistas have been restored, perhaps none better than the sylvan window from beneath the beeches, along the top path towards Mowbray Point, where the breathtaking scale of the whole place opens up. The wooded valley of the River Ure sweeps away far below and beyond you may spy Thirsk, the Hambleton Hills and the distant pimple of Roseberry Topping.

Birdlife here is rich and varied. Kingfisher, dipper, grey wagtail and common sandpiper haunt the river banks. Wood warbler, pied and spotted flycatcher, redstart, woodcock, nuthatch and treecreeper also find the habitat they need in the gorge, along with all three native woodpecker species. In spring the carpets of wild garlic and bluebells are magical. In autumn the golden beech canopy glows up above and the shush of boots through leaf-strewn paths below echoes softly through the damp woodland.

This wood is often wet; the trickle of springs, the gurgle of waterfalls or the deep roar of the river in spate are constant companions and the paths can be muddy. Some judicious tree felling has opened up many of the lost views, while remedial work, rather than total restoration, to many of the follies has retained their original fabric in perfect harmony with the faded glory of this historic park. A low-key approach is the order of the day here. For safety's sake many of the paths have been shored up or provided with new steps, but here and there a few flights of the original gritstone steps survive; the chisel marks of the eighteenth-century stonemasons still evident. Sitting on these old blocks, which feel as much a part of the natural landscape as the crags above, evokes images of those thousands of intrepid Georgian and Victorian 'explorers', most probably ill clad for the rigours of country walking, but still exclaiming and delighting at this 'beautiful wilderness'. Indeed, you can still discover it for yourself today.

OLDBURY HILL

A huge Iron Age hill fort watches over the rolling countryside of Kent

The November sun creeps lazily into the sky, dispersing the morning mists of late autumn, which lounge around the slopes of Oldbury Hill. It's cold, very cold, and the watery sunlight filtering through the woodland, atop this Iron Age hill fort, dispenses little warmth, yet gilds each eastward edge of trunk, twig and fallen leaf alike. It's strange to imagine that more than 2,000 years ago a community lived up on this hill and that they too shivered in early, chilly mornings such as this. They, however, could shuffle a little closer to their fires.

This northern outpost on the Greensand Ridge of the Kentish Weald lies between the M25 and the A25 near Ightham and, if you could still readily see out from the summit, you'd soon realize its strategic importance back around 100BC, when the banks and ditches are reckoned to have been excavated. The hill fort, or more properly the camp, for it is now thought that few of these hilltop settlements had a primary military purpose, is one of the largest in Britain, its ramparts stretching for almost 2½ miles around the hill, enclosing a massive area of

OPPOSITE Sunrise through oaks below Oldbury Hill on a chilly December morning.

The bank in the centre and the dark hollow on the right actually denote the bank and ditch of the hill fort, although a profusion of beech, birch, holly and various conifers rather mask the contours.

about 125 acres. These earthworks undoubtedly could once have provided a first line of defence from less than friendly neighbours or rival tribes. There is evidence that stockades or palisades would have stood along the inner edge of the ditches; probably two lines of sharpened stakes or posts, with an earth infill, perhaps angled outwards against likely marauders. Most historians believe these settlements were often simply used as safe havens for communities and their livestock, many being occupied on a seasonal or occasional basis.

As with so many hill fort sites today, Oldbury shows no evidence of its earthworks from below – it is simply another tree-clad hill in the landscape. A brief, but steep ascent from any direction will inevitably bring you to the distinctive ramparts. Some 2,000 years of leaf mould, fallen trees and rain-washed loam from the bank sides has gradually filled in and partially disguised the ancient ditch, but it is still discernible, although now functioning simply as a convenient terraced path along the hill for walkers. The best-preserved section is along the western

Holly accounts for a large proportion of the ground cover in the wood.

side of the hill, while natural cliffs on the east side performed the defensive function. The remains of the two entrances at the north-east and south ends are still clearly visible.

Excavations around the north-east entrance revealed evidence of a timber gate that had been destroyed by fire quite soon after the construction of the hill fort. Might this have been an attack by Romans? Evidence of human habitation as far back as the Mesolithic period has been discovered on the hill in the shape of several old rock shelters – sadly, damaged by quarrying in the nineteenth century. Many artefacts, ranging from flint implements, hand axes and shards of pottery, have been unearthed over the last couple of centuries.

Walking through the woods brings the strong impression that much of the vegetation is relatively young. Beech groves have sprung up everywhere, some almost certainly self-sown, but much appears to have been planted. A few splendid old coppice stools grasp the ramparts with twisting, toiling roots. Large oaks are the understudy to the beech, but manifest mainly as old, and probably ancient, coppice. The regime has recently been revived in the wood – making this one of a select few Wealden woods once more to be managed in this traditional way. Scots pine, birch and rowan also feature prominently, but almost certainly these have set about their own distribution as and where spaces have opened up in the woodland, rather than having been systematically planted. Much of the ground cover of heather and blaeberry suggests a past of heathland, but this is slowly being crowded out.

A large part of the hilltop has been tamed for farming and a substantial orchard now occupies the ground, but there is still plenty of woodland to explore, following any of the numerous footpaths or ancient trackways across the site. There are viewpoints, but you need to seek them out, as the tree cover right across the hill is generally so dense that it's often difficult to appreciate the sweep away to the north and the Medway Estuary. It is interesting to find a small spring-fed pond in the middle of the enclosure and, assuming this has always been here, a great source of fresh water for any community.

Oldbury Hill is a cracking place to unwind, even though the noise of traffic thrashing along the nearby A25 can be a little intrusive. Best bet is to head away from that side of the hill and peace, tranquillity and the birdsong will transport you.

THE SPIRIT OF INDUSTRY

BENTHALL EDGE WOOD

Embracing the cradle of the Industrial Revolution in Shropshire's Severn Gorge

Winding through the Severn Valley today, around Ironbridge, makes you long to see what this lush and pleasant landscape might have looked like in its heyday. Steeply wooded hills on either side of the Severn Gorge (more recently dubbed Ironbridge Gorge) hem this focal point of Britain's industrial heritage. Although it is believed that iron has been made here since the sixteenth century, a boom period began some 300 years ago, at the dawn of the Industrial Revolution, when the ironworks of Coalbrookdale cast their fiery glow across the valley, followed in due course by the establishment of the renowned china works at Coalport in 1795 and the tile works at Jackfield in the 1870s. Ironbridge was ideally situated, with plentiful local resources of ironstone, clay, coal, limestone and, of course, wood and charcoal from the surrounding woodlands. The River Severn and later on the ready access to the railway network provided excellent channels to get the products out to the waiting world.

Internationally recognized as one of the cradles of technology, Ironbridge Gorge was formally designated a World Heritage Site in 1986. This has all helped to regenerate the area by making it a bustling centre for tourism. Not perhaps what the innovative industrialists of the eighteenth century might have foreseen, but certainly the best way of encouraging inward investment and success to what is now essentially a rural economy. Some of the industries, like Jackfield, have survived as working museums, while others, like Coalport China Museum and the wonderful Victorian town re-created at Blists Hill, are particularly aimed at the tourism market. The centrepiece for the whole region is indisputably the magnificent Iron Bridge, built by Abraham Darby III in 1779, the world's first cast-iron bridge.

From the bridge the view both up and down the river is dominated by the wooded valley sides and to the west, on the south bank, lies Benthall Edge Wood – the largest site of an extensive woodland network hereabouts. The Severn Way footpath leads into the bottom of the wood along the course of an old railway line and soon you can strike up the hillside into the depths of the trees using a choice of excellent paths. One, recently renovated, consists of a very long, winding ascent of wooden steps. Evidence of the wood's working history is all about you, as almost any tree in excess of fifty years old, regardless of species, has been coppiced. Underfoot the earth is black – sometimes this may be due to the remains of charcoal hearths, but often it is simply little lumps of coal emerging from seams which lie beneath the wood.

LEFT The first cast iron bridge in the world was erected in 1779, by local ironmaster Abraham Darby III, and this famous Iron Bridge, spanning the Severn Gorge, has remained a powerful symbol of the Industrial Revolution to this day. The lower reaches of Benthall Edge Wood come right down to the far side of the bridge.

OPPOSITE One of the old limestone quarries at the top of the wood has now become an oasis for ferns, which revel in the cool, damp shade beneath the tree canopy. The limestone was once used as a flux in the iron furnaces below, in the Severn Valley.

The contrast of soil types here is marked. The eastern side, closer to Ironbridge, is mainly acid sandstones with underlying coal; trees such as oak, birch, rowan and wild cherry favour this part of the wood in preference to the western section, where Silurian limestone supports ash, yew, spindle, wych elm, beech, and a few large-leaved limes and wild service trees.

Having puffed and panted your way to the top, there is slight disappointment that all this effort does not immediately afford the views you ought to expect, but several paths lead you onward and just occasionally a glimpse of the surrounding countryside may be caught. Strange hollows and banks throughout the wood reveal activities and boundaries long forgotten and neglected, although most probably relating to a long history of coal extraction. Arthur Young, in his 1776 *Tour of England and Wales*, records that oak coppice from Benthall Edge was cut on a 21-year rotation, the poles barked and sold for use as pit props; the bark, presumably, was sent to the tanneries. As you try to sneak a peek of the valley below, the view beyond the trees suddenly turns mysteriously into a pinkish coloured wall. The simmering cooling towers of Buildwas power station loom unnervingly close and vast. Thankfully, such a massive installation narrowly avoids overshadowing the community of Ironbridge, as it is hidden behind the woods and a gentle bend in the river.

By now you will have reached the western side of Benthall Edge Wood and at the top of the hill you discover substantial quarries, abandoned in the nineteenth century. These great chasms with their sheer rock faces harbour a rich assemblage of mosses, ferns and other shade-loving plants. Several oaks and beeches in particular grasp the lip of the quarry, improbably braced against the elements and a precipitous exit. The limestone has been carted off from these woods for centuries, the last active quarry being the one down the hill, below Pattin's Rock (now a splendid viewpoint over the gorge), which ceased production in the 1930s. The limestone grassland which has grown over the old workings is a riot of colour in spring and early summer; a place to lie on your back amid the fragrant wild flowers with butterflies and bees buzzing busily all around you. The tall stems and impressive flowers of butterfly orchids are a treat in mid-June. If it weren't for the old concrete

The calcareous grassland below Pattin's Rock has grown over what was once the largest limestone quarry on Benthall Edge. Now, in late spring and summer, it is a rich flower meadow with many stunning plants, including this impressive greater butterfly orchid.

anchorages for the tramways which hauled away the limestone you might think you were nestled in some natural landslip. It's always fascinating to see how quickly and effectively nature heals human depredation.

Descending the hill, down towards the river, with broadleaved trees dominating the scene, it's difficult to imagine that in 1837 there were reports of 'thousands of flourishing fir trees' covering Benthall Edge. These may have been pines or even larch or spruce, as 'fir' was often a generic term applied to conifers in general. No matter, there is little evidence of them today.

Benthall Edge is just one of a group of historic working woods around the gorge. However, on the other side of the river, hard by Captain's Coppice, which is once more being actively coppiced with a purpose, lies the Green Wood Centre. There's a growing trend all over Britain for individuals to buy woods to work and enjoy, so the series of courses and lectures on practical woodmanship, conservation and the variety of crafts on offer at the centre are proving extremely popular.

Wherever you walk in these wonderful woods along the Severn, you can't avoid becoming steeped in the rich industrial past of the place. The very ground you tramp is black with ash or coal; remains of pits, kilns and furnaces abound; you can still almost taste and smell the fiery fury of the Industrial Revolution. Yet today you find peace along the valley and, if there's a powerful force at work now, it's nature busily reclaiming the last 300 years.

A shady path along the top of the wood. Careful examination of the plants beneath the trees shows that all their leaves are facing the same way. This is a phototropic response to the nearest source of daylight from a break in the dense woodland cover to the left.

WHITTLE DENE

A secluded Northumbrian valley harbours ghosts of an industrial past

About 10 miles west of the urban sprawl of Newcastle upon Tyne, the north-east of England's premier city, the pace drops away starkly in the sleepy village of Ovingham, where safe and solid gritstone houses and farms squat resolutely above the north bank of the River Tyne. After the breathless cityscape, where woodland is pretty thin on the ground, the tranquillity of Whittle Dene, little more than half a mile from the village, is an idyll sought by many.

A path leads you through meadows to the gateway to the wood and at first all does not look particularly promising. Amid the small stand of conifers which greets you, rubbish drifts in the wind and several recent bonfires have left their scorched scars. Exasperated, you soldier on and, thankfully, the few who seek to spoil it for the many have only managed a very short sally into what is a truly entrancing wood.

Just before reaching the part of Whittle Dene which belongs to the Woodland Trust you stroll among a strange hotchpotch of shacks and chalets, some clearly cherished and in regular use, others neglected and well advanced towards dereliction. There were originally some twenty or thirty of these quaint little refuges in the wood, originally built in the 1920s as healthy bolt holes for the war-weary and battle-scarred after the First World War. Today only eleven of them are still habitable, but their leaseholders are proud if not defiant, and fully intend to keep their little part-time community thriving. Many chalets are painted in bright reds or blues, stamping a stark contrast with their bucolic surroundings, while others rely on more natural greens and browns to slip relatively unnoticed behind their sylvan screens. One communal tap for water and a lack of electricity makes this little enclave one for those who aren't fazed by a bit of basic living.

Constantly accompanied by the gurgling song of the Whittle Burn the trees become broadleaf as you enter the woodland proper. Before long the remains of a substantial group of stone buildings broach the track. On the left you'll discover what once must have been a handsome water-powered flour mill, which apparently ground its last flour about a hundred years ago, and close by the more dilapidated masonry of its erstwhile house, barns and stables. Already this wood is proclaiming its industrial, or perhaps industrious, past. Sitting amid the ruins of a place once so alive, so pivotal in the local economy, but now reduced to little more than a distant memory and a few faded old photographs, musings run close to melancholia, only for the flagging spirit to be rescued by nature. Shrubs and flowers burst from nook and cranny; birds flit this way and that – if you're lucky, a kingfisher skimming the adjacent burn; a red squirrel may peer at you from the safety of the overhanging trees and it is said that otters have been spotted in the river too.

A well-trodden footpath leads you on into the wood, with many branching paths giving you choices to stick to the level-going of the valley or toil up the ever-steepening banks of the dene side. Above the mill there are many of its associated structures still discernible. The millpond is now well and truly overgrown with alder and willow. There is a well, which must once have supplied fresh drinking water for the miller and his family. In the burn there are several beautifully laid stone weirs, used in the past to deflect the flow of water through leats into the millpond. Along the path big stone blocks and boulders, shrouded in earth and moss, are the remains of retaining walls.

All is cool and green beneath the woodland canopy along the Whittle Burn.

Whittle Dene has found fame for its bluebells in spring, being regarded as one of the finest bluebell woods in Britain. Wood anemones and primroses start the flowering season and, as the bluebells wane, the all-pervading stench of wild garlic takes over. Catch it as you stray from the path and the distinctive aroma intensifies and, yes, it is good for culinary purposes, but don't uproot the plants. In this shady, damp defile several ferns can be discovered, including shield fern, broad buckler fern, oak fern and the distinctive hart's tongue. By the burn side you may spot dippers skipping among the rocks or even disturb a heron patiently waiting for a strike.

The wood is essentially an oak and ash mix, but there are also a variety of blow-ins and planted species. Among the former, sycamore is, as ever, doing very well and there are occasional common limes. On higher ground there are some quite impressive beeches – one pollard at the top of the eastern slope may be the best part of 200 years old. Wych elm is naturally occurring, as is the abundance of hazel in the understorey. Both these trees, as well as the oak and ash, respond well to coppicing, and today a local coppice worker is maintaining this traditional practice, which had been introduced several years back by a small group of local woodland enthusiasts known as the Friends of Whittle Dene, with guidance from the Woodland Trust. In the recently cleared compartments it will be interesting to see how natural regeneration picks up on the woodland floor over the next few years. The wood does contain a few conifers – mainly Scots pine and Norway spruce – but the management plan intends to fell some of the spruce and encourage broadleaved species to fill the gaps, whether by planting or natural colonization.

The green glow beneath the dense canopy makes Whittle Dene a particularly magical place to wander in spring or summer. It's easy to lose your sense of time, easy to forget the frantic world somewhere outside, and begin to dream of the miller, the mill-builders, the woodland workers who carved a living from the valley. Suddenly, the cackling of a great spotted woodpecker overhead disturbs you from your reverie, but this is a wood well worth a few visits and you will definitely be back.

OPPOSITE
TOP Nature is slowly reclaiming the derelict remains of the old mill, which was last used to grind flour at the end of the nineteenth-century.

BOTTOM The intense odour of the wild garlic in late spring is truly memorable. Much milder than the cultivated garlic that you buy in the shops, the plant has been used for eons by country folk to flavour their food.

RIGHT
What would British woodland be like without the ubiquitous bluebell? Whittle Dene has a reputation as one of the very best bluebell woods in the land.

CLUMPS, TUMPS, BUMPS AND HUMPS

GAER FAWR

Traces of an ancient community on a Powys hilltop

OPPOSITE An old contorted sweet chestnut along the edge of the upper ramparts of Gaer Fawr hillfort on a glorious spring morning.

BELOW A particularly large sweet chestnut coppice stool on the ascent - undoubtedly one of the oldest trees in the wood.

The narrow country lane that takes you north-west from Guilsfield to Geuffordd, just a few miles north of Welshpool, offers an initially underwhelming prospect of the gentle, tree-clad hump of Gaer Fawr – which means Great Camp. From the outset this is not immediately explainable, but the secret will be revealed. Parking for this wooded hill is an extremely modest lay-by, suitable for only four or five vehicles, so please don't all turn up on the same day.

A couple of paths wind up the hill, and the gradient is fairly stiff, but not overtaxing. Tree cover on these slopes is mainly oak with ash and sycamore – both standards and coppice – with an understorey of rowan, hazel and holly. On the path running up the southern side of the hill it's worth watching out for one particularly large outgrown sweet chestnut coppice stool, which is more than 6 feet across and probably several hundred years old. It's a strange occurrence, as sweet chestnut is not a particularly prominent species in this wood. In spring this ascent is sweetened by the scent of the bluebell carpet all around.

After a while you reach one of those false summits, where you puff and blow a bit, feeling rather pleased that you've made it, before you realize that this is but a halfway lull in the upward toil. Some handsome oaks, birches, rowans and hazels surround the clearing and two huge lumps of oak have been cut

One of the largest wild cherries on the top of the hill.

Oak with stone circle on the summit of Gaer Fawr

into oak-leaf blocks to mark the route, one also acting as a step in the path. Over a low rise you come upon a dew pond, fed by some unseen upland spring. This is an ideal time to pause, mop your brow, and admire the filigree reflections of overhanging branches in the cool, still water. By now you've attained enough height to catch the occasional glimpse through the trees of the countryside far below.

Tempting paths that offer a level option lead left and right, but it really is worth grasping the nettle and forging ever upwards. The softer options around the flanks of the hill reveal clues to the history up here – banks, ditches, ramparts, terraces cut by men more than 2,000 years ago give you the first inkling that this is an Iron Age hill fort. The Great Camp comes into context as you breast the final rise. In spring you are greeted by a splendid clump of wild cherries, their delicate pink canopies billowing over the summit, and tucked in below them a large, single crab apple wafts its honeyed scent on the breeze. Large crabs such as this may not seem particularly old, but they do grow incredibly slowly so that this one may be in excess of 200 years old. The tree is not immediately noticeable in the surrounding woodland, so could this be a descendant of a discarded apple of the Iron Age community? Clearly people have been on this summit recently who hold it special in some way, for a fine open-grown oak in the centre of the fort has

been surrounded in perfect symmetry with a circle of stones. Someone has laboured hard to make this circle. Is this art? Is this a symbol? It matters not. To me, it seems to belong.

The ramparts of this upper part of the hill fort are still remarkably well defined, and looking down the slopes on either side provides ample evidence of the lower defences. Today there are very few places where an unhindered view of the surrounding countryside is possible due to the verdant woodland, thus explaining the lack of archaeological prospect from below. 'Fort' is probably an incorrect term for most of these relics, since the majority were simply hilltop communities; places where people had a commanding view of the surrounding landscape and felt safe from hostile tribes and wild animals such as wolves and bears, and also where they could corral their livestock. Remembering the dew pond, just below the upper part of the hill, makes you realize what a boon this water supply must have been for the ancient community who, in the normal run of events, would have had to transport their water all the way up from rivers and streams in the valleys below.

Wending your way back downhill causes you to ponder what the hill must have looked like 2,000 years ago. Probably far fewer trees, but considerably more people than today.

ERIDGE ROCKS

Amid sandstone boulder and crag in the High Weald of Kent

Weaving through the byways of the High Weald countryside around Tunbridge Wells, that once genteel Kentish spa, hub of the nineteenth century's upper-crust socialites, it's a revelation to discover how much glorious broadleaved woodland has survived to the present day. The Weald has long been regarded as one of Britain's finest and most extensive areas of native woodland; not despite human occupation and exploitation, but because of it.

Iron was already being produced in small-scale bloomeries before the arrival of the Romans, but the demand for greater quantities saw the industry expand dramatically under the new occupation. With a second peak during the sixteenth and early seventeenth centuries, iron production only waned at the beginning of the nineteenth century, when the use of coke for smelting saw the industry migrate to the proximity of large coalfields. A vibrant iron industry needed large quantities of sustainable coppice woodlands to provide the charcoal required for the smelting process. So, despite the mistaken perception of many that chopping down large tracts of trees simply denuded the countryside, the verdant regeneration of coppiced woodland kept the sylvan scenery intact.

Today, the majority of Wealden broadleaved woodland is managed for amenity and conservation. The woodsmen who cut and cleft for fences, gates or hop poles, the skilled weavers of hurdles and baskets, the walking-stick makers and, of course, the charcoal burners have virtually all disappeared. However, the legacy of the woodland economy survives, in what is still one of the most densely wooded parts of Britain, despite ever-increasing demands by agriculture, industry, housing and the transport network.

Eridge Rocks is one of several woodlands around the Kent and Sussex border where the vast bulk of sandstone boulders appear to bubble up through the vegetation, creating giant rock gardens in the landscape. Entering the car park is an immediate confrontation with these impressive outcrops. A main path skirts the base of the rocks, meandering through a delightful secluded valley. Alder dominates the wetter areas around the stream, but the most dramatic sights are the trees which hang from, scramble over or wedge themselves among the rocks. Oak, beech, yew and some fine old hollies have taken their time to coil massive root systems in and around their precarious rocky haunts. Upstart rowan and hazel find any nook and cranny in which to thrive.

By way of a contrast to this natural colonization a few interlopers have staked a claim, almost certainly with the encouragement of the Victorians who loved to come here to ramble and to picnic. A crusty old false acacia seems to be happily growing beneath the rock face, while a handful of pines and larches tower above the lush broadleaf canopy. Remarkably, there can't be too many deer roaming the rocks since both pine and larch appear to be seeding themselves freely … and surviving extremely well. Until recently there was also a great deal of rhododendron here; its dark shading foliage blocking out the light for many flowers, ferns, mosses and liverworts. Sussex Wildlife Trust, which manages the site, has done a great job removing most of it, and as the light floods back in the plants respond favourably.

In the hinterland, above and behind the rock faces, it's a slightly different story. The working origins of the wood are still evident in the abundance of large old sweet chestnut coppice stools, while oak and plenty of hazel complement.

Eridge Rocks does have something of an aura of tranquillity about the place, yet it is also so obviously a site for public recreation, and clearly has been for centuries. Studying the soft sandstone, on top of the

A decrepit looking false acacia, with a burred and deeply fluted bole, grows at the base of the rocks. It is extremely old, and probably a remnant of some of the ornamental planting by the Victorians.

LEFT These oaks have moulded and folded their root systems over and into the contours of the rocks.

BELOW View out across the giant rock garden of Eridge Rocks - introduced pines and larches towering above the native broadleaves below.

OPPOSITE This wonderful old beech appears to be attempting to clamber over the rocks with its far reaching serpentine boughs.

crags nearest the car park, you soon find out who loved who and simply 'who woz here' for perhaps the last fifty years. Anything older has probably eroded away, in much the same way as the people's lives these hieroglyphics record. Slithering down one narrow crevice on some other rocks a short distance away, you may come upon the moss-muted inscription of one 'H.C.', who carefully recorded his (or her) visit on, 'Ap 26 1782'. Today people still walk and picnic here, but it is also a popular venue for rock climbers. Botanists will be rewarded with around 150 different wild flowers on offer.

Looking out from the top of the rocks to the nearby village, I couldn't help remembering when I was a kid. Throughout the year, if the weather was fine (and even when it wasn't), we were out in the woods, building dens, playing Cowboys and Indians, climbing trees and all those kind of things that little lads did in those days. We even had the Cow and Calf rocks of Ilkley Moor a short trek from home, but what wouldn't we have given to have a place like Eridge Rocks on the edge of our village!

VISITING THE WOODS

KEY TO SYMBOLS

Type of wood

Mainly broadleaved woodland

Mainly coniferous woodland

Mixed woodland

Car park

P Parking on site

P Parking nearby

P Parking difficult

Official status

AONB   Area of Outstanding Natural Beauty

SSSI   Site of Special Scientific Interest

NP   National Park

Site facilities

Sign at entry

Information board

One or more paths suitable for wheelchair users

Dogs allowed under supervision

Waymarked trail

Toilet

Picnic area

£ Entrance/car park charge

Refreshments on site

Woods are listed in order of appearance in the book

Castle Eden Dene, County Durham

Follow brown tourist signs on A19 and from Peterlee. Car park off Durham Way. (NZ410387) 222 ha (549 acres). English Nature.

Coed y Rhaiadr, Powys

Take A4059 north at Hirwaun, then left on minor road to Ystradfellte village. Waterfalls car parks on left. (SN932112) 779 ha (1925 acres) AONB, SSSI. Forestry Commission.

Eaves Wood, Silverdale, Lancashire

From A6 follow signs to Leighton Moss RSPB reserve. Continue past reserve on left and take right turn at T-junction. Drive past Silverdale station on the right and continue along road to Eaves Wood car park, approx. 1 km (0.75 mile). (SD465758) 43 ha (106 acres) AONB, SSSI. The National Trust.

Ebbor Gorge, Somerset

From A371 turn at Easton towards Wookey Hole. After 1.5 km (1 mile) turn left up narrow lane towards Priddy. Car park on right after a short drive. (ST525485) 41 ha (101 acres) SSSI. English Nature.

Kingley Vale, Sussex

Turn west off A286 in Mid Lavant (just north of Chichester) toward West Stoke and through village. On sharp left hand bend take right turn. Car park on right. (SU824088) 150 ha (371 acres) AONB, SSSI. English Nature.

Haugh and Nupend Woods, Herefordshire

Haugh Wood is signed 1.5 km (1 mile) from Mordiford Village off the B4244, south-east of Hereford. (SO592365) 375 ha (927 acres). Forestry Commission.

Kingley Vale: the gaping, hollow bole of one of the ancient yews reveals aerial roots dropping down inside. A strange beaked beast or bird appears to be wedged within the tree too.

Bardney Lime Woods, Lincolnshire

College Wood – At Wragby take B1202 south, at Kingthorpe turn right onto minor road signed to Arley. Wood 1.5 km (1 mile) on right. (TF120754) 64 ha (158 acres) Chambers Farm Wood – Take B1202 south from Wragby to Bardney – approx. 5 km (3 miles). Turn left along Hoop Lane and after 1.5 km (1 mile) turn right to wood. (TF149739) 34 ha (83 acres) SSSI. Forestry Commission.

Wye Valley, Gloucestershire

Located to the west of the A466. (SO529059) AONB, SSSI. Various including Forestry Commission.

Bradfield Woods, Suffolk

A134 south from Bury St Edmunds, turn towards Bradfield St George. (TL935581) 73 ha (179 acres) SSSI. Suffolk Wildlife Trust.

Wyre Forest, Worcs./Shropshire

Wyre Forest is well signed from the A456. (SO750739) 1052 ha (2598 acres) SSSI. Forestry Commission.

Denge Wood, Kent

From A28 turn off to Shalmsford Street and, reaching the eastern end of the village, turn right into Mystole Lane and left after 1 km (0.5 mile) into Penny Pot Lane. After 1.6 km (1 mile) the road enters Denge Wood with car parking space on the left. (TR104523) 26 ha (64 acres) AONB. Woodland Trust.

Stour Wood, Essex

From A120 Harwich to Colchester Road turn onto B1352 towards Bradfield. Wood to right of road just before crossroads to Wrabness. Car park off B1352. (TM 190310) 54 ha (134 acres) SSSI. Woodland Trust.

Epping Forest, London

Exit M25 at junction 26 or M11 at junction 5 and follow signs. (TQ412938) 2300 ha (5,685 acres) SSSI. Corporation of London.

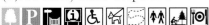

Silent Valley Nature Reserve, Gwent

On A4046 4 km (2.5 miles) south of Ebbw Vale. Leave the one-way system in Cwm on the northern side, turning second left at a brown tourist sign. Car park 400m by Cwm Cemetery. Walk northwards across flat grass playing area and along path to entrance. (SO187062) 50 ha (124 acres) SSSI. Gwent Wildlife Trust.

Bisham Woods, Berkshire

South from High Wycombe on A404 take A4155 to centre of Marlow. At roundabout, take first exit for Bisham. After crossing suspension bridge over the Thames, turn left into Quarry Wood Road. Follow to top of hill then right into Grubwood Lane. Several parking places on right. (SU852844) 153 ha (378 acres). Woodland Trust.

Selborne Hanger, Hampshire

6.5 km (4 miles) south of Alton, between Selborne and Newton Valence, west of B3006. Zigzag path and woods are a short walk from car park in village (adjacent to the Selborne Arms). (SU 742335) 98 ha (242 acres) AONB, SSSI. National Trust.

Burnham Beeches, Buckinghamshire

Main access off A355 Slough to Beaconsfield road, between the two pubs 'The Royal Oak' and 'The Foresters'. Turn into Beeches Road and continue for 400m (0.25 mile). (SU953850) 220 ha (544 acres). Corporation of London.

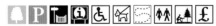

Savernake Forest, Wiltshire

From Marlborough, off the A346 towards Burbage. Postern Hill picnic site signposted off this road. (SU198679) 1000 ha (2472 acres). Savernake Estate managed by Forestry Commission.

Dymock Woods, Gloucestershire

From junction 3 of the M50 head north on minor road to Kempley, then turn south to Kempley Green. Car park on left after 800m (0.5 mile). (SO637285) 501 ha (1238 acres) SSSI. Forestry Commission.

Hayley Wood, Cambridgeshire

From A1198 take B1046 towards Great Gransden. Before reaching the village look for a water tower on right and take track opposite up to wood. (TL294534) 48 ha (119 acres) SSSI. Wildlife Trust for Bedfordshire, Cambridgeshire, Northamptonshire and Peterborough.

Wentwood Forest, Gwent

Take A48 from Newport. Look out for left turn to Park Seymour. Follow road carefully through small village and up hillside to main block of woodland, where there are several pull-ins, a car park and picnic area. (ST412939) 352 ha (870 acres). Various including Woodland Trust & Forestry Commission.

Sherwood Forest, Nottinghamshire

Signposted from M1 and A1 with brown tourist signs. Follow B6034, north of Edwinstowe. (SK626678) 181 ha (447 acres) SSSI. Nottinghamshire County Council.

Glen Affric, Scottish Highlands

(NH284284) 10,000 ha (24,710 acres) NNR, NSA. Forestry Commission Scotland.

Thetford Forest, Norfolk

High Lodge visitor centre signed from B1107 Brandon to Thetford road. (TL811851) 18,800 ha (46,400 acres) SSSI. Forestry Commission.

Glen Finglas, Western Highlands

(NN521108) 4,000 ha (10,000 acres) SSSI, NP. Woodland Trust Scotland. www.glen-finglas.info

High Shores Clough Wood, Lancashire

Exit the A58 Bolton ring road at Moss Bank Park traffic lights onto Barrow Bridge Road. The Barrow Bridge car park is approx 1.6 km (1 mile) along this road on the left. (SD686118) 17 ha (42 acres). Bolton MBC.

The Lochwood Oaks, Dumfries & Galloway

(NY085972) 10 ha (27 acres) SSSI. Privately owned by the Annandale Estate.

Helmeth Wood, Shropshire

Take B4371 east of Church Stretton towards Much Wenlock, first left onto Watling Street South then right fork into Cwms Lane. After 500m (0.25 mile), there is a stile on right with public footpath signs. Follow to top of field and over stile into wood. There is no parking available on nearby lanes. (SO469938) 24 ha (59 acres) AONB. Woodland Trust.

Nant Gwynant, Gwynedd

Park at the Bethania car park in Nant Gwynant on the A498. Wood is on opposite side of road from car park. (SH505625) 30 ha (74 acres). National Trust.

Sunart Oak Woods, Scottish Highlands

(NM748617) 726 ha (1,794 acres). Forestry Commission Scotland. www.sunartoakwoods.org.uk

Kilminorth Wood, Cornwall

In Looe park in large pay and display car park (Discovery Centre) on west side of the river. (SX247538) 46 ha (114 acres). Caradon District Council.

Sea Wood, Lancashire

On the north-west shore of Morecambe Bay, approximately 5 km (3 miles) south of Ulverston at Bardsea. (SD293734) 23 ha (58 acres) SSSI. Woodland Trust.

Tattershall Carrs, Lincolnshire

From A153 Sleaford to Horncastle road turn north onto B1192 at Coningsby. Wood on left after 800m (0.5 mile). (TF215590) 29 ha (71 acres) SSSI. Woodland Trust.

Coed y Cerrig, Gwent

From Abergavenny follow A465 north for 6.5 km (4 miles). Left at Llanvihangel Crucorney, following signs toward Llanthony Abbey. At Stanton turn left and follow Forest Coal Pit signs. Coed y Cerrig is either side of the road, car park on right. (SO292211) 12 ha (30 acres). AONB, SSSI. Countryside Council for Wales, Forestry Commission, Gwent Wildlife Trust

Dimmings Dale, Staffordshire

From Cheadle take B5417 to Oakmoor village, turn right at bottom of steep hill before bridge in village. Take first left and follow narrow lane towards Alton. Car park on left by Ramblers' Retreat Cafe. (SK064434) 260 ha (643 acres) SSSI. Forestry Commission.

Stourhead, Wiltshire

Signposted from A303 and B3092. King Alfred's Tower is 5.5 km (3.5 miles) by road from Stourhead House. (ST748354) 123 ha (304 acres) AONB. National Trust.

Kew Gardens, London

Enter by Brentford Gate via Kew Green and Ferry Lane. Other entrances – Main Gate (off Kew Green), Victoria Gate (off Kew Road) and Lion Gate (off Kew Road). (TQ189768) 49 ha (121 acres). Royal Botanic Gardens Kew.

Westonbirt, Gloucestershire

5 km (3 miles) south-west of Tetbury on A433 Tetbury to Bath road. 20 minutes north-east of junction 18 of M4. Follow brown tourist signs. (ST854900) 240 ha (593 acres). Forestry Commission.

Croft Castle Estate, Herefordshire

From Leominster take B4361 north towards Luston. 3 km (2 miles) after Luston turn left on to B4362. Follow signs to Croft Castle. (SO452656) 52 ha (129 acres) SSSI. National Trust.

Ickworth Estate, Suffolk

5 km (3 miles) southwest of Bury St Edmunds on west side of A143. (TL825619) 236 ha (583 acres). National Trust.

Hackfall, North Yorkshire

Follow A6108 north of Ripon. Take first left after North Stainley through Mickley, and right at T-junction to Grewelthorpe. Wood is situated on the edge of Grewelthorpe, on the road towards Masham. Entrance to wood on right. (SE236771) 45 ha (110 acres) AONB, SSSI. Woodland Trust.

Oldbury Hill, Kent

On the north side of the A25, 5 km (3 miles) south-west of Wrotham. (TQ582561) 62 ha (153 acres) AONB, SSSI. National Trust.

Benthall Edge Wood, Shropshire

From A4169 at Telford take B4373 to Ironbridge. These woods can be accessed from several points along the Ironbridge Gorge. The entrance to Benthall Edge Wood will be found to the west of the southern end of the Iron Bridge.(SJ694032) 270 ha (667 acres) SSSI. Severn Gorge Countryside Trust.

Whittle Dene, Northumberland

Ovingham lies just south of the A69. Park in the village and follow the public footpath which passes beside mill buildings and heads north-west. The path enters the wood at its southern boundary. (NZ072656) 20 ha (49 acres). Woodland Trust.

Gaer Fawr, Powys

From Welshpool take A490 north, then B4392 northeast to Guilsfield. Take last turning left out of village up a hill. Wood on right, with car park at end of wood. (SJ222128) 30 ha (74 acres). Woodland Trust.

Eridge Rocks, Kent

Entrance is via a private road off the A26 in Eridge Green between the church and a small printing works. (TQ554355) 40 ha (99 acres) AONB, SSSI. Sussex Wildlife Trust.

OTHER WOODS TO VISIT

Every Exploring Woodland guide describes and illustrates more than 100 beautiful woods to visit across Britain. Below is a sample selection. Wood name is followed by nearest town, brief description, grid reference and facilities (symbols explained on p196). www.visitwoods.org.uk

THE NORTH EAST & YORKSHIRE

Bitholmes Wood, Sheffield
Urban, upland, ex-industrial (SK293965)

Duncombe Park, Helmsley
Parkland and specimen trees (SE603832)

Garbutt Wood, Thirlby
Characterful oak & birch, natural lake, cliffs
(SE505835)

Hartburn Glebe, Hartburn
River, grotto, folly, bridges (NZ088864)

Irthing Gorge, Gilsland
Ravine woodland, historic spa (NY634685)

Letah Wood, Hexham
Wild daffodils (NY939604)

Mulgrave Woods, Sandsend
Historic landscape including Repton influence
(NZ861125)

Nidd Gorge, Harrogate
Gorge woodland, industrial archaeology
(SE328579)

Ox Close, East Keswick
Working woods – charcoal production plus

grazing regime (SE364459)

Temple Newsam Estate, Whitkirk
Deserted medieval village, ancient trees, urban fringe (SE360320)

Thornton & Twistleton Glens, Ingleton
Limestone ravine woods & waterfalls
(SD695750/ SD700742)

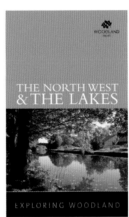

THE NORTH WEST & THE LAKES

Aira Force, Glenridding/Pooley Bridge
Waterfalls, upland alder woods (NY401200)

Alderley Edge, Alderley Edge
History (SJ860775)

Arnside Knott, Arnside, Carnforth
Coastal wood (SD456775)

Bickerton Hills, Bickerton
Clumps & tumps (SJ505530)

Borrowdale Woods, Keswick
'Atlantic' Woods (NY254168)

Claife Woods, Hawkshead
Clumps & tumps (SD385995)

Crag Wood, Meathop
Limestone cliffs (SD457806)

Elnup Wood, Shevington, Nr Wigan
Industry (SD552090)

Formby point, Formby
Coastal wood (SD275082)

Gait Barrows, Silverdale
Limestone pavement, flowers (SD478773)

Haverthwaite Heights, Grange-over-sands/Ulverton
Clumps & tumps (SD342845)

Helsby Hill, Helsby
Rocky hill & heath

High Stand, Armathwaite/Wetheral
Pines (NY498495)

Hyning Scout Wood, Yealand Conyers
Limestone & native limes (SD501735)

Lever Park, Horwich
Historic, formal setting (SD635128)

Moss & Height Spring Wood, Bouth
Oak (SD324863)

Rusland Wood, Newby Bridge
Beech and yew (SD335893)

Storeton Wood, Higher Bebington
Urban fringe (SJ313849)

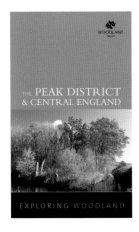

THE PEAK DISTRICT & CENTRAL ENGLAND

Beacon Hill Country Park, Woodhouse Eaves
Clumps & tumps (SK520149)

Bourne Wood, Bourne
Ponds (TF076201)

Bunny Old Wood, Keyworth
Ancient coppice, ditches (SK579283)

Castern Wood, Leek
Native limes (SK120538)

Clumber Park, Worksop
Parkland, specimen trees and lime avenue

Dovedale, Ashbourne
Limestone gorge plus upland woods, splendid flowers (SK145520)

Ecclesall Woods, Sheffield
Charcoal hearths, collier's grave, coppice, beech (SK323824)

George's Hayes, Lichfield
Wild daffodils (SK067133)

Harston Wood, Cheadle
River & alder carr (SK034479)

Hem Heath, Stoke-on-Trent
Urban fringe, great bluebells (SJ885411)

Kedleston Hall, Derby
Eighteenth-century parkland with veteran trees plus lakes (SK313404)

Martinshaw Wood, Groby or Ratby
Great for flowers & broadleaf restoration (SK510073)

Newball Wood, Lincoln
Bardney lime wood (TF082757)

Old Wood, Lincoln
Oak, lime and conifers with flowers aplenty (SK905725)

Padley Gorge, Grindleford
Upland gritstone, millstones (SK251789)

Wharncliffe Woods, Sheffield
Upland wood (SK324951)

Wheata Woods, Sheffield
Uplands & history (SK328943)

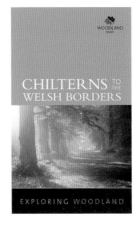

CHILTERNS TO THE WELSH BORDERS

Aston Rowant & Cowleaze, Watlington/Stokenchurch
Ancient tracks, flowers, beech, sculptures (SU726955)

Brockhampton, Bromyard
Parkland (SO687545)

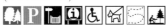

Credenhill Park Wood, Credenhill
Massive hill fort (SO450445)

Fence Wood, Thatcham
Hill fort, views, veteran oaks (SU513723)

Forest of Dean, Coleford
Oaks, sculptures, industrial heritage (SO615121)

Grafton Wood, Grafton Flyford
Ancient lime coppice, oak & ash pollards (SO962557)

Hodgemoor Wood, Chalfont St Giles
Beech and hornbeam (SU967938)

Howe Park Wood, Milton Keynes
Urban fringe (SP831345)

Leigh Woods, Bristol
Urban fringe, limes, rare whitebeams (ST553739)

Little Doward, Monmouth
Superb hill fort, nineteenth-century landscape & great beeches (SO548157)

Mortimer Forest, Ludlow
Ancient lost forest (SO497717 (Black Pool car park))

Penn Wood, Penn Street, Nr Amersham
Wood-pasture, veteran trees and archaeological features (SU914959)

Piggott's Wood, High Wycombe
Woodland industry, beech, Eric Gill connection (SU853987)

Rough Hill Wood, Redditch
Urban fringe (SP052637)

Salcey Forest, Hartwell Village
Ancient oaks, wood banks, flowers (SP795515)

Short Wood, Oundle
Elms & superb bluebells (TL015913)

Wakerley Great Wood, Corby
Fungi, wild service & native limes, archaeology (SP955975)

EAST ANGLIA & NORTH THAMES

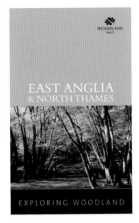

Ashridge, Berkhamsted
Beech (SP971131)

Bedford Purlieus, Peterborough
Native limes, flowers (TL034997)

Broaks Wood, Sible Hedingham
Industrial history (TL784317)

Combs Wood, Stowmarket
Perimeter wood banks & oxlips (TM054568)

Danbury Ridge Reserves, Danbury
Lily of the valley (TL775064)

Felbrigg Great Wood, Cromer
Parkland, massive beeches in wood (TG195394)

Gamlingay Wood, Gamlingay
Oxlips (TL242535)

Groton Wood, Hadleigh
Native limes, lots of ponds (TL977428)

Hainault Forest, Chigwell
(Almost) lost forest, bluebells, ancient pollards (TQ475935)

Hatfield Forest, Bishop's Stortford
Ancient forest, pollard hornbeams (TL547208, TL546199)

Highgate Wood, Highgate
Urban fringe (TQ280883)

Hoddesdon Park Wood, Hoddesdon
Wood banks, ponds, oak & hornbeam (TL348088)

Newbourne Springs, Woodbridge
Swamp alder carr (TM273433)

Overhall Grove, Cambridge/Knapwell
Britain's largest surviving elm wood, archaeology, well, fishponds (TL337633)

Pinmill, Ipswich
Coastal wood (TM206378)

Ruislip Woods, Ruislip
Urban fringe

Tring Park, Tring
Ancient parkland, historic features, chalk grassland (SP927105)

Tyrrel's Wood, Harleston/Hardwick
Plateau alder carr, oak & hornbeam pollards (TM205896)

Wayland Wood, Watton
Coppicing and active management regime (TL924995)

THE SOUTH EAST OF ENGLAND

Ashfield Hangers, Petersfield
Beech hanger wood (SU730265)

Bedgebury Pinetum, Goudhurst
Superb pinetum (TQ715388)

Black Down, Haslemere
Clumps & tumps, beech, pine, heath

Blean Wood, Canterbury
Sweet chestnut coppice wood (TR102593)

Box Hill, Dorking
Clumps & tumps, yew, box, native limes (TQ180513)

Church Copse, Clapham
Bluebells, working hazel coppice (TQ005067)

Dering woods, Pluckley
Oak & hornbeam coppice, flowers & archaeology (TQ900441)

Guestling wood, Hastings
Sweet chestnut, flowers (TQ861147)

Hammond's Copse, Newdigate
Large pond (TQ212441)

Hargate Forest, Tunbridge Wells
Extensive views, stream and ponds, rare flowers (TQ574370)

Leith Hill, Coldharbour, Dorking
Clumps & tumps, beech, pine, oak/birch coppice, natural regen. after 1987 (TQ132428)

Lesnes Abbey Wood, Belvedere
Urban fringe, wild daffodils (TQ478787)

New Forest, Lyndhurst
Ancient forest, oak, beech, heath, etc. (SU300080)

Norbury Park, Leatherhead
Yews (TQ158538)

Slindon Woods, Slindon
Deer park, iron age field patterns, folly, bluebells (SU952073)

Toys Hill, Westerham

Tumps & clumps, beech, fungi, natural regen. after 1987 (TQ465517)

Tudeley Woods, Tonbridge

Charcoal & coppicing – working wood

THE SOUTH WEST OF ENGLAND

Axmouth & Lyme Regis Undercliffs, Seaton and Lyme Regis

Coastal wood, giant landslip (SY332916)

Buck's Valley Woods, Buck's Mill

Coastal wood, oak, Devon whitebeam (SS352235)

Culbone & Yearnor, Porlock

Coastal wood (SS794487)

Dunsford Wood, Dunsford

Wild daffodils (SX805884)

Ethy Wood, Lerryn Village, Lostwithiel

Coastal oak wood (SX136569)

Fernworthy Forest, Chagford

Stone circles, stone rows (SX668838)

Golitha Falls

Waterfalls (SX220687)

Horner Wood, Porlock

Oak, birch, holly & beech, fungi, great views (SS897455)

Kingston Lacy, Wimborne

Beech avenue, Badbury Rings, lime horseshoe, bluebells (ST980019)

Knotts & Parsonage Woods, Newton St Petrock

Old farm, wetland, hayfields, flowers

Shaptor Woods, Bovey Tracey

Rocks, views, oak, industry (SX819798)

Watersmeet, Lynmouth

Step river valley, oak. Whitebeam (SS744487)

WALES

Aber Falls, Abergwyngregyn

Waterfalls (SH671710)

Bishops Wood, Caswell

Coastal wood (SS594879)

Bishopston Valley, Bishopston

Limestone gorge (SS575894)

Coed Cilgelynnen, Fishguard

Alder/willow wetlands (SM979347)

Coed Maentwrog, Penrhydeudraeth

'Atlantic' oak woods (SH655408)

Croes Robert Wood, Monmouth

Coppicing & charcoal burning, fungi (SO475060)

Dinefwr Woods, Llandeilo

Parkland (SN625225)

Elan Valley Woods, Rhayader

Oak woods, water (reservoirs), great views

The Gwaun Valley, Fishguard

Wetlands, spring flowers, archaeology (SN025341)

Gwenffrwd-Dinas, Llandovery

Clumps & tumps (SN788471)

Hafod Estate, Devils Bridge

Old estate, archaeology, river & gorge, beech (SN768737)

Henrhyd Falls, Coelbren

Waterfalls (SN854122)

Lawrenny Woods, Lawrenny

Coastal wood (SN015062)

Mawddach Woodlands, Dolgellau

Estuarine & coastal oak woods, archaeology (SH688192)

Oxwich & Nicolaston Woods, Oxwich

Coastal woods (SS498883)

Pengelli Forest, Eglwyswrw

Oaks (SN130393)

Penglais Hill, Aberystwyth

Urban fringe (SN588821)

The Punchbowl, Abergavenny

Ancient beeches, great views (SO281117)

Stackpole Estate, Stackpole

Riverside & coastal woods, archaeology (SR982965)

SCOTLAND

SCOTLAND

EXPLORING WOODLAND

Ballachuan Hazel Wood, Oban
'Atlantic' wood on coast with hazel a speciality (NM763156)

Ben Lomond, Rowardennan, by Drymen
Coppiced oak, heath , great views (NS359987)

Birks of Aberfeldy, Aberfeldy
River, birch wood, beech (NN855486)

Black Wood of Rannoch, Kinloch Rannoch
Native pine woods (NN617570)

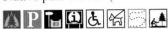

Cambo Wood, Kingsbarns
Snowdrops (NO599106)

Clyde Valley Woodlands, Lanark
Waterfalls, sandstone gorges (NS868445)

Corstorphine Hill, Edinburgh
Urban wood (NT205743)

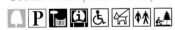

Craighall Den, Ceres
Industrial archaeology (NO399108)

Dawyck Botanic Garden, Peebles
Great tree collection (NT167352)

Dollar Glen, Dollar
Waterfalls, gorge, views (NS964983)

Glen Nant, Taynuilt
Oak woods, industry (NN020272)

Glen Tanar, Aboyne
Native pine woods (NO480966)

Glenashdale, Whiting Bay
Waterfalls and Neolithic cairns (NS030250)

The Hermitage, Dunkeld
Centre of Big Tree Country, earliest larch planting (NO013423)

Ledmore & Migdale, Spinningdale, Bonar Bridge
Huge forest, noted for plentiful juniper, great wildlife and a treasure trove of archaeological features (NH661904)

Mar Lodge Estate, Braemar
Native pine woods (NO097899)

Muir of Dinnet, Aboyne
Birch wood, heath, wetlands, lochs (NO429998)

Ness Glen, Dalmellington
Ravine woodland (NS476014)

Pollok Country Park, Glasgow
Parkland, urban woods, ancient trees (NS560614)

Roslin Glen, Penicuik, Loanhead
Gorge woodland, flowers (NT275625)

Rothiemurchus, Aviemore
Native pine woods (NH898085)

Scone Palace, Scone
Parkland, arboretum, giant trees (NO115265)

Taynish, Tayvallich
'Atlantic' oak wood, wetland, coast wood (NR737852)

Twechar Wood, Kilsyth
Roman archaeology (NS710760)

Uig Wood, Uig
Coastal hazel wood (NG394639)

Urquhart Bay Wood, Drumnadrochit
Swamp alder wood (NH519297)

Yellowcraig, Dirleton
Coast woods, amazing wind sculptured pines (NT518856)

INDEX

ACKNOWLEDGEMENTS

Kind permission from Bloomsbury Press plc to quote from John Berger's
and our faces, my heart, brief as photos.

I would like to thank all the special people who have helped to make this book such a pleasure to complete.

Graham Blight at the Woodland Trust, who originally asked me to write the introductions for the regional *Exploring Woodland* guides and then had the vision to push forward with the illustrated centrepiece for the series, which has become *A Walk in the Woods*. Sarah-Jane Forder, my editor, who kept me on the straight and narrow and curbed my purple departures. Becky Clarke, FL's excellent designer, who has worked her magic. John White for his comments, cues and settling the odd hiccup. Jon Stokes generous (as ever) with his knowledge and particular thanks for his photograph of the Duke of Burgundy butterfly (page 55). A whole string of people who helped with information and support in their specialist subjects or locales: Peter Fordham of Suffolk Wildlife Trust, Sara Bright of Lincolnshire Tree Awareness Group, Jim Helps, Paul Jackson at Coppice Creations, Rick Vonk from RSPB, David Lovelace, Ian Tyres, David Brown at Queen's University in Belfast, Jon Winder at Wentwood Forest and many WT site managers from around the country (you know who you are). All the team at The Darkroom in Cheltenham. My partner, Jan, for her encouragement, patience and love. Lastly, the Scotties – Phoebe and Molly – who love woodland walkies.